with best regards —

Lewis Behler

TM

Guild Press of Indiana, Inc.

Indianapolis, Indiana

Back Home Again

By

Louis A. Bibler

Guild Press of Indiana
6000 Sunset Lane
Indianapolis, IN 46208

Guild Press of Indiana, Inc.
6000 Sunset Lane
Indianapolis, IN 46208

Printed in the United States of America

Library of Congress
Catalogue Card Number
93-079617

ISBN 1-878208-27-6

TABLE OF CONTENTS

Title   **Page**

Acknowledgment and Appreciation

Without the gentle prodding of that perfect secretary, Donna Carr, I never would have bothered to transfer these memories from my head to paper. And without her cheerful and repeated labors at the word processor, my scribblings would not have been converted to a legible manuscript.

Without the advice and support of writer-friends James Opie and Spencer Gill, the manuscript would not have been retrieved from the "Maybe Someday" file.

Finally, let me thank John Gallman, Director of Indiana University Press and J. Kent Calder, Editor of the Indiana Historical Society's *Traces* for keeping me on a trail which led to Guild Press.

The author's share of net proceeds from the sale of this book to January 1, 1999, are pledged in equal parts to Indiana Historical Society, Acres, Inc., and two other entities.

Dedication

To grandson Sam, with a reminder that today will be yesterday tomorrow; and that nothing can be accomplished yesterday.

In Memory of Daddy and Mother

*and those enchanted days of early childhood
with my reasonably peace-loving siblings,
Jean, Robbie, and Charles
On our beloved Spring Brook Farm,
Jay County, Indiana.*

GREEN HILL SCHOOL

Author—3rd from left in second row, kneeling; Brother Robbie—2nd from right in front row; Brother Charles—4th from left in second row, kneeling; Teacher, John McFarland.

1922 Photo Courtesy Dallas May

CHAPTER I

UNCLE BARNEY AND FRITZ

For some reason our "black sheep" Uncle Barney and our little fox terrier dog Fritz seem to share a common relationship in my earliest memories. This relationship is mainly temporal, in that they occupied the same time span in my childhood, although they did have another commonality—both were "loners."

Our Uncle Barney was not really a black sheep, more appropriately a medium gray one. He was my mother's brother and his real name was Timothy. The origin of the nickname Barney was never explained, but given his antisocial bent, it is understandable that he may even in his early youth have been deemed to be less than housebroken, hence a "barnie." Come to think of it, not only was he not housebroken, he was not even outhouse broken. I can still see him on a winter day carefully selecting a matched set of corncobs from the kitchen woodbox, then glumly heading out the door and down the snow-covered path to do his back-of-the-barn toiletry. Our outhouse apparently was too civilized for him—or too busy.

At any rate, in the earliest recollections of us children he was an on-and-off resident at our house. He occasionally occupied space there, and space is about all you could say for the room in which he bunked. It was the back room upstairs which was used to store odds and ends of things too big or too small to store in the adjacent "crawl space" over the kitchen. It was, incidentally, the room in which we children used to spread walnuts and hickory nuts to dry—and to noisily crack and eat there, leaving a crunchy litter of shells on the floor. This fact alone could explain why Uncle Barney's stays with us were sometimes abruptly terminated of his own choice.

It seems strange in retrospect to realize that the room had no clothes closet, not even a clothes hanger or a coat rack. This absence of common conveniences was not due to lack of space, as the room was quite spacious. It must have been that Daddy was not really keen about encouraging Uncle Barney to settle in, and therefore deliberately omitted putting in a closet or clothes hangers. Uncle Barney's personal furnishings were only an old trunk and a large tin barrel, painted green. These items were an attractive mystery to us, like a pirate's treasure chest; and we did not hesitate to explore them for treasure. About all we ever found were some rumpled old clothes, some empty Prince Albert cans and an empty El Havana cigar box or two; and over everything floated the overwhelming reek of tobacco.

Uncle Barney, constantly spare and gaunt, lived almost entirely on peanuts and cookies, a diet which seemed nearly perfect to us kids at the time and one which really appealed to our dog Fritz, also. To call Fritz "our" dog is misleading. Fritz was his own dog—a dog's dog, if you will. Like Uncle Barney, he was by choice a loner, and never, never were we able to get him into the house. The closest we could ever come was by making a trail of peanuts leading from the back step, through the open screen door and into the summer kitchen. Fritz would eagerly follow this trail, consuming it as he went, but would never proceed farther than halfway across the threshold, thereby always keeping his hind feet planted on his own turf. As a last resort we would slam the screen door on him, trying to force his rear end to follow his front end, but even this treacherous tactic proved unsuccessful. It could be asked why we simply did not pick him up (a small fox terrier) in our arms and carry him inside, but no one who had ever tried to pick Fritz up for any reason would pose such a question. The South Carolina state motto "Don't Tread on Me" was tailor-made for Fritz.

Perhaps because of their mutual bond of peanuts and cookies, or perhaps because they both sensed they were loners, Fritz and Uncle Barney were often seen together, sitting in the sun on the back step or on the running board of Uncle Barney's old Ford. This vehicle, a recalcitrant starter, was a prime source of entertainment to us children—not the car itself, but Uncle Barney's efforts to crank it into action and then to keep it going. These side-splitting exertions and accompanying monologue of expletives would be priceless today if only they could have been captured with a camcorder; unfortunately memory will have to suffice.

Whenever we would see Uncle Barney on a cold winter day fill a bucket with steaming water from the kitchen range reservoir or teakettle, we would troop along silently after him to watch the show. As a preliminary step, Uncle Barney would remove from the hood a thick mulch of old automobile "side curtains," old quilts, even bundles of corn fodder and place over the radiator grill a hand-fitted section of cardboard. Then he would unscrew the radiator cap and optimistically pour in the bucket of steaming hot water. By this time his nose, always inclined to drip, would require serious attention, so he would blow it on the ground, one nostril at a time, using alternate thumbs on alternate sides. After carefully adjusting the spark and gas levers on the steering post, he would take the crank from under the seat and make his way to the crank-insertion point below the radiator. Uncle Barney always walked in a sort of modified Groucho Marx crouch, taking long steps, with hesitation between, as if to get a little bonus glide; just to watch him ambling around the car up to this point was getting us dangerously close to the giggle point. But the show was yet to come.

First he would give the cold, stiff motor a few half-turn cranks, as if to just get its attention. Then he would firmly re-set the crank and his feet, and with a muffled growl give it a four-revolution spin. When nothing happened, he would grumble the first tentative curse, saunter to the door to carefully readjust the spark lever, and make his way back to the crank, his nose now dripping unattended. Seizing the crank, without any more preliminary spins, he would rotate it furiously, gasping out a single word of a lengthy curse on each up-cycle. By this time we would be looking at each other or holding our hands over our mouths to keep from giggling too loudly, and over our ears to keep from hearing too much. After several repetitions of cranking and spark adjustment, the engine would be warmed up enough (either through friction or Uncle Barney's body heat) to catch a spark and give a few sputtering coughs. Seduced by these signs of life, Uncle Barney would make bow-legged lunges for the spark and gas levers, only to have the engine die just as his fingers were within inches of success.

These failures would goad Uncle Barney into such torrents of cursing and such furious spinning of the crank that we would be virtually rolling in the snow, while Fritz

ran around barking and sniffing the air in search of the cause of all the commotion; and Uncle Barney would have had enough company. Making a run at us with the crank, he would send us scurrying for the house, where we would have to be content to watch his automotive antics from the safety of the dining room window. It is small wonder that Uncle Barney was not a permanent occupant of our house and that even Fritz viewed our company with some skepticism, therefore devoting most of his time to dog stuff.

Fritz thought it his divine duty to rid the world of rats and snakes. He felt strongly that the only good rat or snake was a dead rat or snake. In dealing with snakes, had he lived in Ireland, he would have made St. Patrick redundant. He would literally shake a snake into fragments. Seizing the poor creature in the middle, he would so violently whip it from side to side that centrifugal force would snap the snake into two pieces. Then Fritz would repeat the maneuver with each piece until the multiplied segments were too short to snap, say six inches. Only then would he stalk away, having made another "good" snake— in fact several of them. It has occurred to me that he may have been encouraged in this vendetta by our father, because in the old days Daddy was a bit unenlightened in his attitude toward snakes. This was an era wherein snakes, weasels, skunks, "chicken" hawks and most other nonfood animals were lumped into the category of "varmits," thus subject to extermination. We children were encouraged to vigorously pursue with stick or hoe every snake we encountered, regardless of the fact that none were poisonous, and all actually were beneficial to the farm ecosystem.

Although snake control was high on Fritz's agenda, the extermination of rats was his main occupation, and one which he pursued with fanatical zeal. On a good day Fritz would have inert rat bodies strewn around the corn crib like a Texas version of enemy casualties around the Alamo. No rat was too big or too small for Fritz, although he did not eat them. He would just shake them at about sixteen G's, then when they were too dizzy to stand, would shift his grip and audibly crush their bones without breaking the skin. Fritz was a professional. He had a scar on his nose as a reminder of the time he had reached in to pull a "possum" out of a stump. From that time on, no opossums ever needed to play dead around Fritz. They already were dead.

But like the rest of us, Fritz was not completely happy to be doing what he did for a living, and aspired to bigger and better things—things outside his reach. What he really wanted to do was catch a rabbit. This may not seem like an overly ambitious goal, as dogs are supposed to catch rabbits, and it seems only natural that Fritz not be denied this canine right. So he pursued, in full cry, every cottontail rabbit which ever took flight in his presence, although never catching a single one. But he never gave up hope. On his last day with us, at ten years of age, he gave his usual maximum-effort, full-throated chase after a rabbit in the clover field in front of our house. Shortly thereafter he was found, as if quietly dreaming, in his bed in the woodhouse. Although that was his last day on earth, it would be nice to think that somewhere Fritz still dreams of continuing his lifelong effort to catch up with at least one of those fleet-footed little cottontails—like Wile E. Coyote dreaming of catching the Road Runner.

CHAPTER II

UNCLE BARNEY'S BARBER CHAIR

One day early in the years of his intermittent stay at our house Uncle Barney was seen unloading a barber chair and carefully setting it up about fifteen feet from his car, under the big cottonwood tree. The layout of our lane, barnyard and driveway was such that a car coming from the lane could turn to the left into the barnyard or turn to the right, between two huge, spreading cottonwood trees, into the driveway leading to the garage. Uncle Barney's car was always parked under the one of these trees which was immediately to the left of the driveway. Then immediately to the left of his car is where he unloaded and set up his barber chair. I make a point of this layout because exactly where Uncle Barney set up his chair that hope-filled day in 1923 is where it was to remain for several years.

Uncle Barney's barber chair, winter and summer, was a fixture of our landscape, although it was kept under such a multilayered thatch of protective materials that it was not easily recognizable. However, once or twice per year Uncle Barney would remove layer by layer this protective mound of tattered binder canvas, oil cloth and burlap bags to reveal in all its nickel-plated splendor his gleaming treasure—his hope chest. After sitting in his chair and giving its elevating lever a tentative pump or two, Uncle Barney would renew the above embalming procedure, as if deciding that the time for launching his career was not yet quite right. Then he would crank up his car and drive off to Salamonia to pick up a couple tins of Prince Albert and a paper poke each of cookies and peanuts.

Maybe to hone Uncle Barney's tonsorial talents or maybe just to save money, Mother appointed Uncle Barney to be the official barber to us children—much to the dismay of all participants. These barbering sessions were always postponed as long as possible, but eventually we were trapped into haircuts. For some reason no consideration was ever given to using the grand, shiny barber chair out under the cottonwood tree. Instead, we were seated on top of both catalogs stacked on top of our high kitchen stool. Here we were draped in a flour sack dish towel and told to sit still. Then Uncle Barney, with his used set of hand operated clippers (and no previous experience) would vengefully set to work.

I can't remember that he ever used a comb or scissors, and his clippers were so dull that his operation was based more on force than techinique. He would grasp his squirming young client's head like a melon within the spread of his big left hand. Then he would set the clippers firmly at the nape of the neck and force the head and the clippers painfully toward each other. The resulting swath of hair bunched in between the dull clippers and the barrier formed by Uncle Barney's left thumb would eventually fall to the floor, leaving a zig-zag, white path in the wake of the clipper. These zig-zags were due to the fact that hand-operated clippers cut hair on squeezing the handles together, and are supposed to cut also on the spring-driven return stroke of the handles. However Uncle Barney's dull, second-hand clippers would cut hair only on the squeeze and would pull hair on the return. The result was a cut-pull, cut-pull effect which caused the client to jump about an inch off his seat on each return stroke of the clipper.

It was an excruciating and patience-testing business for both parties, but one which held the attention of us spectators like morbid viewers of an old-fashioned hanging. I can still see Uncle Barney at work, a smoldering hand-rolled Prince Albert cigarette dangling from his lips and one of our doomed heads clamped firmly in his left hand. He always positioned the outside edge of his left thumb to be the lower rim of the "haircut," much as the edge of the bowl would have served in the proverbial "bowl haircut" of our day. Then he would grind the clippers toward his thumb, flexing his jaw muscles with each squeeze of the clippers for all the world as if he were chewing the hair off at the roots; and that's what it felt like, also. With Uncle Barney there was no touch-up trimming or talk of a little more off here or there. When his cut swath on one side met the point of beginning on the other side, the job was done. And on this pronouncement the client scrambled instantly from the stool area like a shorn sheep from the shearing deck.

However, for some reason the newly shorn ones were soon back at the scene to bedevil the unfortunate one still on the chair (and thus the barber). Verbal taunts would soon lead the bedevilers to physical sallies into the danger zone, like Indian braves counting coups. At first Uncle Barney would only growl admonitions and threats at these tormentors, but inevitably, at least once in every haircut session, things would reach a physical level. Uncle Barney's most severe and effective punishment was "knuckling." Eventually one of us tormentors would be caught by a sweep of that horny left hand, the clipper would be laid down, and the poor wretch be placed in a headlock under Uncle Barney's left arm. Then those bony knuckles of his right fist were employed in a knuckling of the skull so severe that despite apologies and promises of saintly conduct forevermore, the haircut party usually would end in a flood of tears—and a sobbing, "I'm g-g-gonna-tell-Mother on-on you-oo-OO!"

But I am sure we managed to get even with Uncle Barney. There were all kinds of ways we could find to devil him. Like the time he was getting ready to shave and had put some water to heat on the kerosene stove in the summer kitchen. There were no chairs out there, so as soon as he lit the burner he went to the kitchen to sit down and read the paper, while waiting for the water to heat. Well, this seemed too good to pass up, so to my everlasting shame I slipped in and turned the wick down and blew the flame out then turned the wick back up.

After a few minutes, Uncle Barney went out to the stove and after a bit of muttering, checked the fuel tank, re-lit the burner and retired again to the kitchen. Observing this from outside the screen door on the back step, I repeated my skulduggery. This time Uncle Barney got into some pretty serious cursing before lighting a different burner and shifting his pan of still cold water. Now getting pretty nervous, I dowsed his fire once more then left the area completely, being terrified of the consequences if caught. I did notice hours later that he was clean shaven, but thought it best not to bring the subject up.

Uncle Barney worked off and on at a sawmill in Muncie, and one time he came home proudly displaying a brand new invention, the safety razor. It was the first one we had ever seen, and of course we were all eager to see it demonstrated. It wasn't often that Uncle Barney found himself the center of such an admiring audience, and so he agreed to let us watch his first shave. Actually he didn't have much choice, because the only room in the house with water and a mirror was in the kitchen. This was the scene of all washing, shaving, even Saturday night baths until we reached the age of embarrassment, which fortunately was about the time we were big enough to carry a washtub upstairs.

Anyway, we soon were all gathered around Uncle Barney as he stood before the kitchen mirror all lathered up and ready to take that first stroke with his glistening new Gillette. For a while it appeared that something might actually work out for Uncle Barney. But alas, success once more was to elude him. That first stroke drew blood and a curse. And so did the second. And the third. At first there was some snickering, but as the blood and curses reached ever increasing volume, the snickering soon stopped. Uncle Barney, unwilling to admit that he might not yet be ready for advanced technology, plowed ahead, sticking a little scrap of newspaper on each new cut until you could have read half the day's news right on his face. By this time we were too embarrassed to watch any longer, and it was weeks later that we found that he had placed the blade on the outside of those two little guards, and therefore had finished an entire shave with a bare and unmounted safety razor blade. It's a wonder he didn't bleed to death.

Mother and Uncle Barney had a sister Nora (Norrie) who lived at Neptune, Ohio, near Celina. Here Aunt Nora and Uncle Louis (Lute) ran a crossroads country store, and once or twice per year we used to visit them. This was always the big trip of the year for us kids, as it was a distance of thirty miles from home. It was so far, in fact, that Daddy was reluctant to go there "in the machine," and so sometimes Uncle Barney would volunteer (or be volunteered) to take us.

As soon as word of a motor trip reached us children,

we immediately spoke for "sides," the equivalent of window seats on a plane. "First on the right side!" "First on the left side!" This of course was the end of the sides, so the two who had not taken the initiative could only whine something like "That's not fair. You had the right (or left) side last year." Speaking in advance for firsts was a big thing to us kids. We even spoke for positions in "washing feet." "First washing feet!" "Second washing feet!" After second it didn't make much difference, because the foot water would already be pretty thick by that time, anyhow. It was the same way with taking a bath, back in the days when all four of us shared a communal batch of bath water. Come to think of it, we even spoke in advance for the best piece of chicken or the best piece of rabbit. "First on the pulley bone!" or "First on the middle piece!" these being the wishbone of a chicken and the loin of a rabbit respectively. You had to be on your toes around our house, lest you find yourself forever in the middle seat of life's "machine," eating ribs and necks.

When we learned that Uncle Barney was to be our chauffer to Aunt Nora's, we immediately went on our best behavior around him, because much was at stake here. Not only was Aunt Nora the best cook in the world, but Uncle Lute ran a combination barber shop and convenience store, which included an ice cream bar. And if that were not enough, we would get to see the Celina Reservoir, by far the biggest body of water we knew. It was, indeed, the big trip of each year. Thirty miles!

In preparation for the trip, Uncle Barney could be seen patching up all his spare inner tubes, filling the radiator, and checking his supply of Prince Albert, peanuts and cookies; and then we were off, leaving the farm to Daddy overnight—much to his relief, I am sure. About as far as Daddy liked to drive our machine was three miles to Salamonia to Sunday church, or maybe eight miles tops to the stock yard at Portland, with a veal calf in the back seat.

Uncle Barney, on the other hand, was to us children a world class automobile driver, having driven many times to Muncie and even once to Indianapolis, where he attended the Indy 500. "Not much to it," he said. "They go so fast—just zoom, zoom and they're gone." Anyway, we did not much care who did the driving to Aunt Nora's as long as somebody did.

This internal peace of mind was a good thing for us, because Uncle Barney's driving would not have won any awards from today's driver training instructors. His car was a Model T sedan of around 1920 or so, when sedans were built almost as high as they were long, like the pictures of the old Toonerville Trolley. This made them so top-heavy that they lurched along on rough roads like the old stage coaches. Therefore, it was always a relief to get off our mud and gravel township roads of Indiana and onto that engineering marvel, a concrete highway in Ohio.

On this smooth strip of concrete, Uncle Barney could roll his cigarettes without interrupting the journey, and we could all experience the thrill of smooth highway travel—or we could have, except for one automotive peculiarity of Uncle Barney's. He seemed to think, despite much scientific evidence to the contrary, that there may be such a thing as free energy; or maybe even an element of perpetual motion. At any rate, that endless ribbon of smooth concrete stretching out ahead of him seemed to bring out the idea that he should be able to coast down the road without using the engine—except just to build up to exit speed. It does seem logical, all right—that if the earth is round, then that highway should always be going down-hill, once you get on top of the curve, of course.

But apparently we never reached that downhill point, because for mile after mile all the way to Celina, it was the same formula: rev up the engine and roar down the road until reaching a ground speed probably around forty-five MPH; then clutch to the floor, gas lever up to the top we would sail along in silent splendor for about a hundred feet, before optimism would have to give way to the laws of physics. Then when we were about to go into a stall, out with the clutch, down with the gas lever, and we would lurch and roar into neck-snapping, piston-powered acceleration again. We must have sounded like a propeller-driven airplane with an intermittently clogging fuel line.

But none of us ever once questioned Uncle Barney about this automotive procedure. After all, he had been to the Indy 500, and besides we were interested only in travel for travel's sake, not the mode of transportation. All too soon, it seemed, we had reached that vast body of water, the Celina Reservoir, where we were moved by emotions probably similar to those of Balboa when first viewing the majesty of the Pacific Ocean. From Celina it was but a short drive (or coast) to Aunt Nora's house at Neptune. And even as we turned into the driveway: "First on the right side on the way home!" "First on the left side on the way home!" "Aw that's not fair. You can't speak already for sides." "Yes you can. As soon as you get there you can speak for sides!" So there I was, shut out again by swift action and cold logic. I did start to speak for "first washing feet," then realized that we had our shoes on so would not be washing our feet. Oh well—maybe next year.

CHAPTER III

SEARS AND ROEBUCK CATALOG
AND THE HUCKSTER WAGON

It was actually Sears, Roebuck and Company, but we always called it Sears and Roebuck, maybe because we could envisage two nice, whiskery old gentlemen like the Smith Brothers who made the cough drops. Some called it the Wish Book, but to us children on our Indiana farm of the twenties and thirties, it was much more than that—it was our main reason for working and gave specific and concrete incentives to the work ethic. What better reason to work for children and parents alike than to accumulate the money to "send away" to Sears and Roebuck for some long-dreamed-of treasure pictured on a well thumbed page of "the catalog."

More than the source of all things needed, it was our window to the world. It was an escape from those sometimes too familiar walls of our house and barn and a trip to a fabulous land, a land where anything ever desired by anyone on earth was available. Not only was it available, but also in the very size required by each person, and in three grades, ranging from "good" through "better" and "our finest quality." There was something satisfying and flattering, even snobbish, about being able to consider choosing the "finest," as if that put the barefoot, grubby shopper right up there at the top—as if maybe the Prince of Wales was considering purchasing the very same item at the very same time.

It has been said that firewood warms twice, once in the chopping and again in the burning. Another good old

homily is that anticipation is as good as realization. Well, the Sears and Roebuck catalog could have inspired both those old sayings and more. Many more.

First there was the arrival of the book itself, an occasion around our house ranking right up there with Christmas. After all, where did Christmas presents come from? Somehow word would get around the neighborhood that the new catalog was about due, and from then on we would be watching up the lane for the rural mail carrier to come in sight. It was a quarter mile from our house to the mailbox, so we did not walk to the mailbox unless we saw the mailman pause at the end of the lane. Then one of us kids, by pre-arrangement, would make the trip to the box and bring the catalog to the house. There it would be opened on the floor, so we could all read it together. Following some bickering over what to "look at first," our inspection would proceed in reasonably orderly fashion through toys, books, skates, sleds, BB guns and eventually into heavier stuff of group interest, such as horse harness.

One good thing about harness was that the better and best sets were shown right on the horses—beautiful, spirited teams of dapple grays, legs prancing, nostrils flaring, ears cocked forward—all this just for the "better" quality. "Our finest quality" harness not only would picture a team of horses from a Currier and Ives painting, but would also have the Currier and Ives hip-roofed barn and collie dog. The horses would be hitched to a new wagon and were sweeping at a trot along a curvilinear driveway, between luxuriant fields of corn and toward the open door of the distant barn. The inference to be gleaned from this portrayal of "our finest quality" was either that it was designed only for the most prosperous farm or else that once acquired it would bring the pictured prosperity to its fortunate owner. At any rate, if I knew where to buy such a set of harness today, I would be tempted to buy it just for prosperity insurance.

Daddy actually did order a new set of harness one time, and although it did not bring us great wealth, it certainly did bring us children lots of satisfaction. Those yuppie types of today's generation, who boast of the smell of their new cars, unfortunately have missed out on the real thing—the smell of a new set of harness! Ours probably was not "our finest quality," but it was fine enough to remain more memorable to me than my first automobile. It had beautiful brass knobs on the hames, and lots of brass studs and rivets, but best of all that wonderful new-leather smell!

Along with the set of harness came a five-gallon drum of harness oil, and we kids were soon put to work oiling not only the new set, but also the old set. To do this we poured some of the oil into an old wash tub, then dismantled the harness strap by strap and dipped it and rubbed it while holding it over the tub. When we had finished, the new set did not look and smell quite "brand new," but the improvement in the old set made up the difference. Needless to say we soaked up almost as much oil on ourselves as did the harness; but the harness picked up enough oil that our faded old gray mares, Maud and Molly, were as striped as zebras for weeks after the harness oiling.

In "shopping" for any article of clothing which Mother could not make, we pored over the catalog. Shoes were a big item. You did not simply one day say, "I need a new pair of shoes", or "I am going to order a new pair of shoes." Far from it. First you struggled along with your old shoes (probably handed down to start with) until they had been half soled at least once. This was done by Daddy on a heavy steel cobbler's shoe tree with its set of steel "lasts" ranging from baby size to adult size. This cobbler's set itself had been ordered from Sears and Roebuck, along with assorted slabs of leather and shoe nails. For many years Daddy's "do it yourself" cobbling forestalled the absolute need for each new pair of shoes for as long as possible.

At any rate, when half soles were flapping on the floor with each step and new shoes were a must, then it was time to get out the catalog. But selecting that pair of new shoes was not a thing to be rushed, but a thing to be savored—as the selection of a fine wine. First you went through all the shoe pages alphabetically from "baby" to "woodsman," then gradually zeroed in on your own general group. Then came the choice of color, and last the choice between "good," "our better quality," and "our finest quality." It was not a thing to be taken lightly. At last the order was placed in the mailbox and the flag turned up to alert the mailman to outgoing mail. Then commenced the days of real anticipation.

For the order to go to Chicago by rail, be filled, then returned by rail was really no longer than the average mail order today, with all our jet planes and computerized space age "progress." Within a week or ten days, the mailman would pause at our mailbox and the one of us who had placed the order would hurry to retrieve the parcel and open it up. Here again one did not rush things. First to be savored was the cigar smoke odor of the exterior of the package. Cigar smoke was exotic to us because very few farm folks ever smoked cigars. Then from the inside of the package would come the rush of product smells—in this case new shoe leather and maybe even shoe polish. If the shoes were "everday" shoes, they were immediately put on and worn with that special pride reserved for "new" things, which were very uncommon in our lives. If the shoes were dress shoes, they were put away for "Sunday," later to be worn self-consciously and often protestingly on feet yearning for their usual barefoot freedom in the open fields.

It would serve no real purpose to attempt to list the categories of products available from the catalog, because it can all be summed up in the expression, "everything from A to Z." This is not to say that you could send off for an aardvark or a zygote, but only because these two items were not in trade anywhere. If they were not listed in the Sears and Roebuck catalog, they were just not available. Its list of merchandise was amazing, and amazingly well organized, and farm life memories of the twenties and thirties would have been greatly diminished without this wonderful book.

Useful beyond description as a shopping center, the catalog had other uses probably not foreseen even by those visionary and foresighted original partners. It was the first choice as an elevating seat for the baby, for flattening a mouse, as a temporary prop under broken furniture, or as a spelling guide or memory reminder. But most of all it was a toilet commodity without which farm life would have been much more abrasive. As soon as the new catalog arrived, the old one was transferred to the outhouse, which in our case was called the closet. It had seating accommodations for three, sized large, medium and baby, with the baby size thoughtfully stepped down to baby height. The mind's eye automatically jumps to the picture of a basic family of three, sitting there in a row, gazing pensively out over the chicken lot. This, of course, is not the way it worked in real life. However, it seems such a logical notion that if I were designing one even now, I think I would size it the same way, like the beds of the bear family in "Goldilocks and the Three Bears." At any rate in our "closet" and in almost every other outhouse across the land the used Sears and Roebuck catalog was the toilet tissue of custom. And also with the annual introduction of the "new" used catalog, every outhouse across the land became truly a restroom, even a defacto library—at least in summer time.

Here, to the contented clucking of hens, the monotonous chattering of English sparrows, and the companionable buzzing of flies, the occupant could rest at leisure—as time stood still. Although generations following that halcyon era may not be able to recognize any benefit in brousing through one's toilet tissue in situ, as it were, those catalog pages had many fringe benefits over the single-purpose commodity of today. Much as we had studied the pages of the catalog during the previous year, more yet remained to be gained through review. Here we could spot that Flexible Flyer sled which had so thrilled us months before on Christmas morning. There we would catch the familiar pattern of the oilcloth which now covered our kitchen table and remember all over again that unique new-oilcloth smell which pervaded the kitchen for days after we had unrolled it on the table.

Section followed section, each differing from the others. In the woven-wire fencing section could be found beautiful pastoral scenes, with pigs, horses and cattle all grazing together in perfect harmony alongside such a caption as "Pig Tight, Horse High and Bull Strong." In contrast to these landscaped sections, and inevitably more popular with pubescent young farm boy occupants of the outhouse library would be the women's wear section. Here, with intent concentration, those rather prim and stodgy corset-staved figures could be made to foretell the bikini of today; and that utilitarian and strait-laced old catalog could become a virtual *Penthouse Magazine.*

As weeks and months drifted by, page after page, then section after section, gradually were used up until toward year's end pickings were becoming thin indeed. One by one even the glossy pages began to disappear, portending the approaching moment of truth. But about this time the new catalog would appear at the mailbox, and the old one would appear at the outhouse, and the partners Sears and Roebuck would have seen us through one more year on the farm.

The Huckster Wagon was not in direct competition with Sears and Roebuck for the reason that it provided mainly a barter system which exchanged store goods for eggs. It came every week, and every week we kids had our noses glued to the dining room window to catch it turning into the lane. We then announced its arrival so that our cases of eggs could be carried out, and so that we could all be ready to participate in the event. To us, particularly in the winter, it must have been like the docking of a trading schooner at a remote island, our farm being that island.

The wagon itself, by the time I was old enough to remember it, was actually a store built onto the "running gears" of a Model T truck in archetypal motor home manner. It was a completely rectangular affair, custom-made

of wood, with slatted chicken crates built-in on both sides. Protruding necks of startled chickens barely cleared the rutted roads in winter time, and above the chicken crates were solid tiers of egg cases. When seen coming down the lane, the rectangular Huckster Wagon looked like a giant egg case itself and moved along at a very sedate pace indeed, the driver being fully aware of the fragility of its cash cargo.

When the vehicle had been backed carefully up our driveway and the doors opened up, we children would jostle for the best positions on the wagon step in order to see and smell everything inside. On the inside the Huckster Wagon offered a veritable treasure trove of goodies. It was a rectangular cornucopia on wheels!

Before commencing his grocery list, the grocer-driver, in the earliest days Russ Messner, would visually add up the number of eggs already cased, then if there were additional eggs in a bucket or basket, would case those and compute the total value at perhaps ten cents per dozen. (In those days the standard egg case held thirty-six dozen—432 eggs—and "egg case" was as common in country language as six-pack is today). After counting the eggs, the grocer would get out his order book, and while writing the order, would keep a running tab of Mother's purchases. As she approached the end of her list, he would let her know how her egg credit was holding out, so that she could add or subtract items to fit.

The Huckster Wagon actually was a miniature general store. It had groceries, dry goods, hardware, drugs, even kerosene, which could be drawn into our five-gallon kerosene can from a tank. Coal oil, we called it. Mother's purchases were generally such things as Fels Naptha soap, bluing, toothpicks, matches, bananas, crackers, vanilla, salt, spices, sugar, flour, aspirin or cough medicine, cotton dress goods, thread, and just maybe five or ten cents worth of candy or a ten cent ring of bologna. This was an old fashion ring bologna which I have never seen anywhere except in Indiana, and we children were crazy about it— probably because it was full of garlic and other flavorings which were never used in our home cooking.

When Mother's list was completed, the grocer would settle the bill with her, then swing our cases of eggs above those already tiered up on both sides of his wagon, drop off empty cases, crank up the wagon and creep away down the lane to the next house. This was an important and efficient service to our farm neighborhood, and its weekly visits were memorable events to us children during pre-school and early grade school years. Our farm family, and most others around, were almost entirely dependent on eggs and cream for day-to-day cash. The cream we sold weekly at the "cream station," three miles away in Salamonia; but it was the eggs which attracted that portable general store, The Huckster Wagon, to our door. So who needed a shopping mall?

CHAPTER IV

BUTCHERING DAY

When I go back to memories of childhood on an Indiana farm, I feel sorry for the children of today. I feel sorry for them because most will never experience the seasonal rhythms of that simple life which we lived so close to the earth. It is true that children of today do participate in Christmas, Thanksgiving Day, Fourth of July and various other holidays, also important to us back in the twenties. But there is no way they can participate in many interesting and nostaligia-provoking events experienced by farm children generations ago.

Such eagerly anticipated events as butchering day, cider-pressing, molasses-pressing, apple butter-making, threshing day, nut-gathering—all had their special charms—which indelibly impressed the events on childhood memory. The fact that many of these were related to harvesting and preparation of seasonal foods may have accentuated those memories. If so, how sad it is that today's children will be able to look back only to supermarkets in search of similar or equivalent childhood memories.

Butchering day, usually on a Saturday and following snow in early December, was presaged by certain additions to the routine of our father's daily chores. We would see him doing such things as grinding butcher knives and the axe on our old grindstone. This foot-pedaled, eccentrically worn disc of sandstone stood under a big cottonwood tree about halfway between the house and the barn and was a common indicator of events to follow. In summer the grinding of a sickle-bar for either the mower or the binder was an ominous portent of hot, sweaty, itchy field work to follow. But in December, seeing Daddy at the grindstone evoked visions of butchering day activities, and the smell of fresh tenderloin, sausage and liver sizzling in the skillet, and fresh cracklings from the lard press. The final indicator that butchering day was imminent would be to find the butchering pole placed across two saw horses out behind the woodhouse. And on the pole the two big, black iron kettles, flanked by newly chopped wood. We knew then that butchering day would come tomorrow for sure.

At breakfast the next morning, over Post Toasties or Quaker Oats, the talk would be of how many hogs we were going to do and who would be coming to help. This help usually was a trade with neighbors or relatives. Many aunts and uncles lived nearby, and all were good butchering day help and fun to have at the job. Henry Stover was our favorite neighbor helper. With his ready grin and his friendly way of "kidding us kids," he was a welcome guest. After he had helped fill the big kettles with water, stoked the fire again with wood, and neatly tucked a chew of Mail Pouch into his mouth, he would turn to Daddy and say, "Well, Charlie, are we about ready to make some meat?"

Then away we would troop toward the barnyard, Daddy leading with his little, worn out Stevens Crack Shot .22, and Henry with a sticking knife, Charles, Robbie and I following. Scampering impatiently among us would be our old fox terrier dog, Fritz. Although a veteran of many butchering days, Fritz never tired of the annual event. No doubt his enthusiasm, like ours, was heightened by visions of the impending change in menu associated with the .22 rifle, the smell of wood smoke, and the hustle and bustle of the big day. At the barn we would pick up either

Molly or Maud, already harnessed, and hitch her to the little flat bottomed sled we called the stone boat. Then we would go to whichever hog house contained the pigs that had been kept "at home" when all others had been shipped off to market.

As Daddy slipped a .22 short into the rifle and took aim between the eyes of the vaguely suspicious pig, all talk would cease, much as when a critical putt is being lined up at a golf match. In the ensuing hush, the miniature crack of the .22 short, and the instantaneous, stiffed-legged drop of the unlucky pig were stark drama to child onlookers. Even more dramatic would be the instant reaction of Henry Stoner, who with one swift probe of the sticking knife would release a great, hissing gush of crimson onto the bedding of the pig pen.

Somewhat sobered by this sudden end of the life of one of our erstwhile barnyard acquaintances, we would lead a now wide-eyed and snuffling Molly to the hoghouse door. Here, as one of us held onto the bridle of the now suspicious Molly, another tugged the mute and quivering body of the pig onto the little sled. Then, with one leading Molly, we others would follow the snow-flattened trail of the little stone sled through the hog lot gate, through the barnyard gate, and on to the butchering site behind the woodhouse. Enroute, the sled trail through the snow would be tinged with crimson, reminding us of its quivering but lifeless cargo. On reaching the butchering site, however, our dampened spirits were revived by the sight of steaming kettles lapped by the flames of the wood fire and the smell of wood smoke.

At this point the pig would be heaved with much puffing and grunting off the stone boat and onto the scalding platform, at one end of which the scalding barrel was

positioned at a low angle. This scalding platform was actually the remains of a large, home-made sled used for hauling corn fodder from the fields through the snow of winter and the mud of spring thaws. We called it the mud boat, and it seemed quite natural and not worthy of mention that the pig would be offloaded from the stone boat onto the mud boat.

Once the pig was in position for scalding, boiling water was carried in pails from the kettles to the scalding barrel and a shovelful or two of wood ashes was added. A meat hook was inserted behind the hock tendon of one hind leg, and the pig was slipped headfirst into the barrel, with two men on the meat hook handle keeping the animal in motion during the scalding process. After a minute or two of dunking the carcass, Daddy would say "let's have a look," and the pig would be slipped out far enough for scraping tests to be made. If the hair slipped easily, the carcass would be reversed, and the process repeated. When completely scalded, the hog would be slid all the way out on the platform by a big concerted heave. Like a car from a car wash, the hog was now a clean and shining red, white or black, depending on the breed.

At this point all hands, including the children, would participate, working away companionably with bell scrapers, corn knives, or simply pulling out the warm, steaming hair in handfuls. In remarkably short order, the once familiar Duroc Jersey, Poland China or Chester White would have been converted into bare and impersonal pigskin ready for hanging on the meat pole, where it would be washed and "dressed out."

Before the carcass was hung, one of the men would delicately excise the male sex manifestation from the carcass. If Henry Stoner performed this surgical act, he would hold out the product in front of us kids and say "Now which one of you gets this?" When we would recoil with demurring giggles, he would turn to a tail-wagging Fritz, hovering expectantly nearby, and say, "Well Fritz, it looks like its all yours. At least it will keep you busy for a while." And so it did. A half hour later, Fritz could be seen lying in the weeds, still optimistically chewing away, tilting his head first to one side, then the other, as if in search of the sharpest set of molars. By this time word had traveled the feline grapevine also, and the house cats and later the barn cats had assembled on-site. As a result, each nearby fence post and chopping block had a furry, ornamental finial. There they would sit, silent and round-eyed as owls, expectantly awaiting the actual dressing procedure in hopes of windfall benefits.

For hanging, a "spreading stick" would be inserted behind the hock tendon of each hind leg. This spreading stick was then used to lift and suspend the carcass upon the pole for "dressing," which meant removing internal organs. As a matter of courtesy, this technical part of the procedure would be offered (and accepted) in turn by Uncle Walter, Henry Stoner or Daddy, each one as proficient as another.

As if it were yesterday, I can see the entire procedure from start to finish. First a slit was cut in the rubbery portion of the snout, then two fingers of the left hand were inserted in this slit for a firm grip, while with the right hand the razor sharp butcher knife encircled the neck, cutting cleanly to the vertebra. Then with a sharp upward and backward pull the neck vertebra would separate with an audible pop and the head would be lifted and plopped into a waiting dishpan.

But this was just the beginning. Before our admiring eyes, the vent would be cut free and tied with binder twine, preparatory to the bold stroke which would open the belly skin of the hanging carcass from top to bottom. The climactic moment came when the entire mess of entrails could be dropped, completely intact and steaming, directly from the hanging carcass into a dishpan held by Aunt Dora or Mother who up to this point had been busy in the kitchen. So while the men (and boys) returned to the hog house to repeat the outdoor work, the women's work commenced.

One major and unforgettable element of this work was "cleaning the casings," as it was delicately termed. "Scraping the guts," as it was indelicately termed, was not a job for the faint of heart, particularly the first step, which was to strip the intestine of original contents. This step, needless to say, was conducted outside, preferably in private. Mother, Aunt Dora and Aunt Lulu all were proficient in casing preparation, although none of them looked forward to it. I remember quite plainly observing their individual reactions to the afore mentioned first step. Mother, always on the quiet side, expressed only a rather pained smile. Aunt Dora, a jolly, pink-cheeked woman, made a laughing joke of it. Aunt Lulu, Daddy's red-haired and outspoken youngest sister, was openly vitriolic in her on-the-job comments. It probably did not improve her mood that we would be sure to utter a loud and complaining "peee-yew!" everytime we came near her. "P-e-e-e-yew!"

After removal of casing contents, water was scooped into one end of the casing and stripped through and out the other end several times. This operation was conducted outside also. Subsequent washing and the actual scraping were completed inside in dishpans, on a scraping board. This board was known (of course) as the gut board, and was carefully saved and used year after year. Continued use had given it a velvety texture important in preventing the casings from being perforated when subjected to several on-the-board scrapings with a table knife. The finished product was as thin and translucent as tissue paper and was exhibited quite proudly by each individual who had a hand in the process.

By lunch time (dinner time, we called it) two or three hogs were hanging like marble statuary on the meat pole, and we all sat down to a feast more memorable in its own way than Thanksgiving. In addition to the usual staples and trimmings of "company" dinner were those long-awaited platters of freshly fried pork loin, liver, and brains. Although I have dined in some of the world's best restaurants, I remember none of those dinners so fondly as the dinners on butchering day, when we were kids on our Indiana farm.

Sausage and lard-making usually occurred the weekend after butchering, and were closely associated operations, in that both products were made from meat trimmings. Following butchering day, after the meat had cooled out and stiffened, Daddy would take down the wide, smooth meat boards from their storage place on the garage rafters, set them on sawhorses in the garage and start trimming out the hams, shoulders and sides of bacon. Because in those days cholesterol was completely unknown, all butchering hogs were big and fat, around three hundred pounds. Trimming out the hams and shoulders, therefore, resulted in great chunks and slabs of fat. These were thrown into baskets for lard, and the trimmings containing some lean meat were thrown in separate baskets for sausage. When the hams, shoulders and bacon were all trimmed out, Daddy would rub these with a thick layer of salt, brown sugar and pepper mixture and put them aside for smoking.

Rendering lard was a mild, gentle sequel to butchering day, held outside and utilizing the same big iron butchering kettles, still suspended over the ashes of the butchering fire. Not much help was required, and we usually would do the job within the family.

The procedure was to cut the fat scraps into one inch cubes, dump them into the big kettles and build up the fire. Soon the fat would begin to sizzle and melt on the bottom of the kettles, until eventually the unrendered cubes would be floating in boiling, liquid fat. This boiling process was continued, the mixture being constantly stirred with a long wooden paddle, like a canoe paddle. Toward the end the skin and fiber of the cubes shrank into crisp cracklings, giving off a heavenly fragrance. These could, and would, be fished out and cooled, then crunched down in an annual ritual which unfortunately has no taste parallel today. (Those abominable pork skins in snack packages at the market do not even give a hint of what a newly cooked crackling fished from the kettle, or better yet hot from the lard press, used to taste like!)

When Mother or Daddy declared the lard cuttings to be completely cooked, the fire was raked away so that the contents of the kettles could cool sufficiently to permit ladling the mixture into the lard press. The press was a sturdy iron cylinder-shaped container with a spout at the bottom and a movable lid at the top. This lid was attached to a spiral screw, so that it could be cranked down with great force on the contents of the container. This ingenious device was mounted on a board, and this board we laid across two big blocks of wood, convenient to the kettles of hot lard. As children our job was to sit on both ends of the lard press board to hold it down while Mother ladled in the hot lard and Daddy turned the crank. Ours was the perfect job, right in the middle of the action, but with none of the exertion. Watching the crystal clear, filtered lard flow from the press spout into the five-gallon lard cans, breathing in the heady fragrances of wood smoke and roasting pork rinds, crunching on freshly pressed and still hot cracklings—what could be more fun for a child, particularly a hungry one? Nothing in the world.

Sausage-making, although interesting, had neither the drama of butchering day nor the instant satisfaction of rendering lard, but was a memorable part of butchering, nonetheless.

The meat for sausage consisted mainly of trimmings from hams, bacon sides and shoulders. The casings, which had been so carefully scraped and cleaned during butchering, were kept in an earthen jar of salt water until sausage-making time. This actual sausage-stuffing was usually conducted one evening after supper. The preparation was headed up by Daddy, who seemed to remember seasoning requirements from year to year. The sausage was ground in our hand-cranked meat grinder and, as in lard-pressing, it was our job to sit on the ends of the grinder board, laid across two kitchen chairs, while Daddy turned the crank.

Watching the chunks of meat being converted to sausage and popping out the little holes in the end of the grinder like a swarm of pink and white worms was almost hypnotizing, and soon we had half a washtub of ground sausage ready for seasoning. Daddy used only salt and pepper, which he kneaded into the ground meat with his bare fists. When he had it sufficiently mixed, Mother would flatten a few small patties into the skillet on top of the big wood-burning kitchen range, and in no time we were sampling the seasoning of our new batch of sausage! It always tasted wonderful to me, and I would give anything to try it again.

After the sausage was tasted and approved, the lard press and the casings were brought in, and we once more sat on the press board observing the miracle of sausage-stuffing. First the press would be filled with big, double-handed gobs of sausage meat and the press lid closed down over it. Then Mother would thread several yards of casings on the spout of the press and pinch the casing end together and Daddy would start turning the crank. It amazed us kids to see the sausage meat flow into the casing, which would seem to take on a life of its own, coiling smoothly around and around the bottom of the tub in glistening coils like a fat, pink-mottled snake. The first few blowouts of a casing would be the cause of near-hysterical laughter on the part of us kids but were not greeted with equal merriment by Daddy. We soon learned, therefore, to restrain our outbursts to muffled giggles. All too soon the process would be over, and the tub of sausage carried out to the garage to keep cool.

Within a day or so, Mother would put on a big cold-pack canning operation with about half of the sausage, and Daddy would fire up the smoke house to smoke the other half. We would use the smoked sausage directly from the smoke house trays, and of all the home-prepared meats of my childhood, that is the one which tops my four-star memory list. Home-made, hickory-smoked sausage!

CHAPTER V

KANTNER'S WOODS AND THE CRAWDAD CREEK

For reasons which I can not quite put on paper the woods and streams of our Indiana farm were always dearer to us as young children around six, seven, eight or nine years than were the house and other buildings. This preference I can only attribute to a theory that instinctive feelings for habitat were developed over millions of years of our evolution. If this theory were true, it would mean that these feelings must be stronger than those developed during the last few thousands of years wherein artificial and unnatural structures were our habitat.

This is not to say that we did not appreciate our house and all associated buildings, which incidentally had the following not very catchy names: new chicken house, old chicken house, chicken-lot chicken house, woodhouse, old kitchen, garage, barn, toolshed, old hoghouse, new hoghouse, and corn crib. In addition, of course, there was that all-important building, the outhouse, which we always called the closet. It is only to say that when around the buildings, we dreamed mostly of getting down to the woods or the "crick," whereas when at the creek or woods, we had to be called back to the house—unless hungry or cold, of course. Some of our preference for outdoor locale may be due to the fact that there were lots of chores and responsibilities associated with the buildings and none with the woods and streams. It may be that simple. At any rate, we were "woodsy."

At the south end of our farm was a relatively un-
spoiled eighty acres of timber owned by our neighbor, Jesse
Kantner. Because of the great size and density of the trees,
the ground was shaded in this woods to such an extent that
it could not support the usual bluegrass of the neighboring
pastures nor the ragweeds and other annual weeds of the
nearby cultivated fields. Therefore the ground cover in
"Kantner's Woods" was early flowering perennial plants—
which we knew as wildflowers. In early spring we children
frequently made our way back to Kantner's woods to gather
wildflowers to bring home to Mother.

The route we followed to Kantner's woods was an
adventure in itself. From the house we went down the hill
and across the creek, then up the opposite hill by way of an
ancient wagon road. This old road trail was worn about
three feet deep into the hillside but completely grassed
over for scores of years, like present day traces of the wagon
trail of the forty-niners on the western prairies. The trail
led directly to a two-room log cabin, probably unused since
around 1850. It had been framed on ash and oak log sills set
on rocks and was traditional lath and plaster interior,
sided with black walnut outside. It had a slab roof overly-
ing unpeeled pole rafters. In our childhood it was a ghost
of a building, with an empty door and empty windows, and
was only used as a shady rest by our sheep.

About fifty yards beyond this old house under a
giant elm tree was a fresh-water spring, which no doubt
had attracted that first early settler to this homesite back
in the eighteen hundreds. Sometimes we would gather
clay from around the spring, take it to the ghost house and
make mud pies, which we would leave to dry on the open
window sills. (What a shame it is that we eventually tore

this building down without even taking a photo or digging into the records to trace its history.)

From the spring we would follow a little intermittent stream on southward through our pasture to Kantner's woods. Here we would slip between the ineffective strands of an ancient barbwire fence and after going only a few steps would enter another world. Instead of newly greening pasture grass, on the ground was a thick spongy mulch of leaves and leaf mold, interspersing patches and beds of wildflowers. Along the stream which flowed from the woods toward our spring were scattered beds of violets (johnny-jump-ups, we called them). These were found in three separate colors—blue, yellow and white, but all with that same heavenly fragrance. Equally fragrant were what we called sweet williams (wild phlox) and these grew in large beds. All around us and overhead the great, gray boles of oak, ash, hickory, maple and beech towered toward the sky, and through their now-bare branches the early spring sun barely dappled the ground. As we scampered around under these trees, attracted from flower to flower like roving bees, we were soon so far into the woods that we would become worried and then would make our way back to our familiar fence line to look out on our own pasture land. Thus reassured, we would once more lose ourselves in gathering flowers, first this one then that one of bluebells, buttercups, dutchman's breeches (lady britches, we called them) and many others for which we had no name.

So haunting are memories of the fragrances of the various flowers and of the bursting tree buds, the damp leaf mold, accompanied by the trilling calls of mating birds and the wild, free beauty of the entire scene that they come back to me often. I can see the four of us now, with our hands so filled with flowers that they kept slipping away from us, finally causing us to head back to our line fence, across our bluegrass pasture, past the spring and the old cabin, across the creek and up the hill to the house. Here we would proudly present our flowers, now sadly wilted and frazzled, to Mother. She would exclaim over the beauty and fragrance of them, placing them in glasses of water on the kitchen table to recover, while we told her all about the wonders of Kantner's woods. To my knowledge she never saw Kantner's woods herself. Like Daddy, she was always too busy taking care of the four of us—and other farm animals and farm chores.

Daddy did find the time, one day when the four of us were still very young, to take us down to the creek and show us how to fish. We had acquired new lines, hooks and bobbers from somewhere, but did not know how to use them, so he helped us dig worms and put them in one of Uncle Barney's Prince Albert tobacco cans, then with his pocket knife cut some slender willow limbs and rig up our poles. He then took us to the west end of our creek, where it was joined by a larger branch from the south. Here we tossed in our baited hooks, and wonder of wonders, immediately caught fish! It was a new world, and all ours! We had stumbled upon the Meaning of Life! Nothing else need we know, ever.

After showing us how to put our fish on a stringer and telling us to go no farther than our own fence line, Daddy left us to fish and went back to his work, never again to fish with us. But then we did not expect him to fish with us. Fishing was for children, not adults. Adults were not supposed to do fun things. When we could wait no longer we took our string of little shiners up to the house to Mother, who told us how nice they were (probably just what she needed) and helped us cut their heads off and clean them. Then she put a skillet on the stove, rolled our little fish in flour, explaining that the scales would not bother and fried them really crisp like smelt. She told us we could eat them bones and all as long as we ate plenty of bread at the same time. And this we did, and they were delicious.

We continued to fish that same hole for days, taking along a bucket so we could take our fish to the house alive, until we had it pretty well fished out. Daddy then told us we would have to wait until we had a big rain causing the water to rise and bringing more fish up the creek to our fishing hole; and he was right. However, while waiting for more fish to come, we found that crawdads could be almost as much fun and were in more plentiful supply.

For some reason crawfish were not considered to be edible in our part of the country, so it never occurred to us that our playground, the Crawdad Crick, was literally crawling with a Cajun staple and delicacy. Our crawdads were an unending source of entertainment, and there was one under almost every rock in the creek bed. They were particularly numerous in the area receiving the flow from the south branch, at the extreme west edge of our farm. And this is where the four of us could be found in the summertime.

There were a great number of shapes, sizes, and colors of crawdads, and on lifting a rock, one never knew what might come scooting out—a blue one, a red one, a soft-shelled one, a big mama one with a cluster of eggs under her tail. Better yet, a mama with a cluster of babies under her tail, each a perfect miniature of an adult. Some-

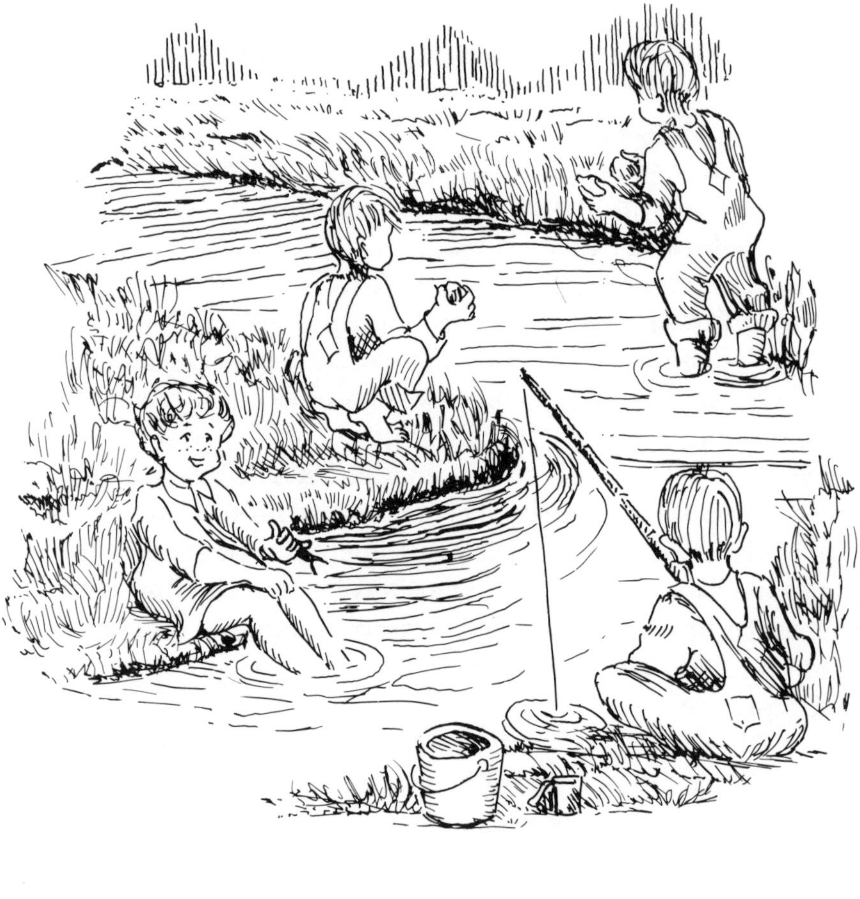

times it was not a crawdad at all, but a beautiful little red-striped fish called a johnny darter. Sometimes it was a leech, a slippery, black, ribbon-like creature of which we had no fear at all, never having been taught they are harmful, which they were not. In fact, after an hour or so of wading in the water, it was routine procedure for us to pull the leeches off our legs before going to the house.

We never tired of this area of murmuring riffles and shallow, wadable pools. Because it was a part of our livestock pasture, the sheep kept the grass trimmed like a lawn and kept the entire area free of weeds and brush. At the south end of our playground was a group of wild grape vines of ancient origin, climbing to the tops of surrounding trees. These provided not only swings, but also "chairs" and even a crude "trampoline" on one laterally sprawling trunk. Our Crawdad Crick playground had everything we needed, even drinking water. Although the creek no doubt drained upstream barnyards for miles, we had our own theory that "moving" water was safe to drink, and so we always drank from the riffles. The people at the Environmental Protection Agency may not subscribe to this theory—but what do they know? It worked for us.

CHAPTER VI

INDIANA CORN

Anthropologists say that the cradle of civilization in the Tigris-Euphrates Valley was built around the harvesting and subsequent cultivation of a wild grass called dinkel, the parent of modern day wheat. Well, the Mesopotamian culture may have been built on dinkel, but our Indiana farm culture was built on corn, a gift of the American Indian, and developed from a wild grass called teosinte. It wasn't actually a gift, but more like a theft from the Indians, as was certainly the Indiana land on which we grow it.

One of my earliest recollections is of going afield on a warm June day with Mother to take Daddy a drink of water. He was plowing (cultivating) corn in a field near our lane, and the corn was just then up about four inches above the ground, in neat cross-checked "hills." These rows of hills could be traced across the field, seemingly to infinity. Because the rows were "check" planted, they were seen as rows no matter in which direction they were viewed, as are the rows of a checkerboard or the knots on a homemade "comfort."

The rich, fertile smell of the freshly cultivated earth and the dramatic, moist, earth-color contrast of the freshly tilled rows to the drab, dry gray of the untilled rows are impossible to forget. I remember the soft snores of relief emitted by Maud and Molly as they would cock a hip and settle down in their joints for a two-minute horse-nap. Between drinks of water from the fruit jar, Daddy would tell Mother we had a "good stand" of corn and he hoped to "get through it" to knock the weeds out before the next

rain. Mother would say dinner would be ready at noon—
"fried ham, mashed potatoes, ham gravy, creamed peas,
and strawberries." Daddy never carried a watch—never
owned one on the farm—and for a good reason. "Appointment" was an unknown word in farm language. "Noon"
was good enough for dinner time, because all the township
roads and all the fence lines in our region ran north-south
or east-west, and when fence post shadows pointed north
it was noon. Back at the house Mother put two of us picking peas and the other two to picking strawberries.

Our lives revolved around the cultivation of corn.
Ours was a corn-hog economy. Wheat, oats and soybeans
were incidental crops. Wheat actually was seeded mainly
as a cover crop for red clover, which was grown for the next
year's hay, then plowed under for the big crop—corn. A
good crop of corn is a beautiful thing to see, and every stage
of its growth was impressive to a child. The actual check
planting procedure continued to mystify me, and I considered Daddy to be really special, if for no other reason than
that he could accomplish this mystical process. In fact, my
most dreadful and most frequently recurring fear was that
something would happen to Daddy and none of us children
would know how to plant the corn. "Whatever would we
do?" It was here that I would envisage all of us plodding
down the road to that often threatened "Poor Farm." Life's
dreams and fears were simpler then. Fortunately, Daddy
continued to live until I found other worries to replace that
one of who would plant the corn.

Corn in that warm, humid climate of Indiana grew
so rapidly that it was our childhood equivalent of bamboo—or better yet the beanstalk of "Jack and the
Beanstalk." There were "old timers" who said they could
hear it grow. As a child I used to listen for these growth

sounds, but never could say for sure that I heard them. But I certainly can say that after a warm rain in early July, I could feel it grow and I could smell it grow. It smelled like the cobs of freshly cooked corn-on-the-cob—the entire field of it.

As children we sometimes used to make our way back into the middle of a field of tall corn and pretend we were lost in a forest. It was actually kind of scary, with no visible landmarks and no human noises—nothing but the pervasive rustle of blade on blade and the occasional chirp of a cricket or the distant crow of a rooster. We would stay until one would suddenly break for the outside—then all would go in a somewhat more than make-believe panic. Once started, we would not stop until having burst out into the open sunshine, panting from exertion and smarting from corn blade scratches and cuts on our bare arms and faces, half ashamed of our inner panic.

The corn was our calendar, our almanac, and a major item of our childhood conversation. It was time to plant corn "when the elm leaves were as big as squirrels' ears." Corn "knee high by the Fourth of July" was a saying so common as to become almost universal. Our neighbor and butchering friend, Henry Stoner, was always the first in our community to plant his corn, an early-bird practice which Daddy sometimes deplored, saying that Henry often had to replant. But among men getting your corn out earliest was something like what getting your wash out on the line earliest on Monday morning was to women—a prestige thing.

Long before we children were old enough to use the corn plow (cultivator), we were sometimes deployed in the field to hoe out the weeds which had escaped the cultivator. If we grumbled about this, Daddy would console us by telling us horror stories of how rough it was for kids when he was a boy. For example, they (all thirteen of them) were put out into the fields with wooden mauls to "bust" clods in preparation for planting. I always visualized this as a sort of chain gang operation, featuring "Granpap" as overseer, with a shotgun. Then their planting itself (presumably when all the clods had been busted) was done by hand, either with hoes or hand planters—"jobbers," they were called then. And as to early-day weeding, almost all this was done by hand-hoeing, because tree stumps were so thick as to make plowing impractical. Well, by the time we had heard about these slave labor conditions of Daddy's childhood, we felt pretty lucky to be chopping only the odd weed in a double-cultivated checked planting, believe me.

Corn-growing created an ever changing calendar of the seasons. In early spring, a newly plowed field epitomized the promise of Mother Earth. To walk barefooted behind Daddy as he turned those smooth ribbons of clover sod with a walking plow was unforgettable. I can still feel under my feet the cool, moist earth of the furrow bottom, planed smooth by the plow share. I can hear again the muffled snapping of innumerable clover roots, the rythmic creaking of harness leather and the squabbling of blackbirds and robins as they prospected the newly turned earth for worms. I can smell the rich, organic fragrance of humus, as the crumbling skeletons of decaying corn stalks buried by a plowing two years previously were now exhumed and laid down by the mold board as recognizable corn-fossils within a matrix of dark loam. I can still see the plowshare and mold board, hypnotically turning the clover stubble upside down into parallel wrinkles, seemingly extending to the horizon, as in a Grant Wood landscape.

Working the plowed ground with disc and harrow,

although it destroyed the furrowed pattern left by the plow, replaced it with a velvety seedbed landscape which had its own ephemeral charm, in sudden transition from corduroy to velvet. And from the time of emergence of the geometric pattern of those first green shoots from that nurturing seedbed, this newly created landscape was constantly changing. Appearance of the sun after each June rain was an invitation for a barefoot inspection tour of the cornfield to "see how much the corn growed."

By mid-July, delicate golden silks and lavender tassels were bursting forth from the lush green stalks, and from then it was only days until "roas'in' ear" time. Why we always referred to corn-on-the-cob as roasting ears is not clear to me, because we never roasted them, although we practically lived on boiled green corn in season. We grew Country Gentleman and Golden Bantam sweet corn in the "truck patch," but ate field corn just as readily after the sweet corn was gone. Sweet corn, sliced tomatoes and new potatoes were daily fare for three weeks in late July and early August when we were children. And the piles of frazzled corn cobs which accumulated on the worn oil cloth by each of our plates as dinner or supper progressed was phenomenal.

Cornfields were the site of another gustatory delight equally memorable to us children—the melon patch. Watermelon and muskmelon patches were located in the cornfields for two reasons, both good. One reason was that within the limits of one field or another, could be found just the proper type of rich, sandy soil perfect for melon culture. The other was that only within the protective screen of a forest of corn stalks could melons be hidden from the forays of melon-hungry children. For neighboring children, locating and raiding each other's melon patches was a

Sunday afternoon pastime second to none. Best fun of all, of course, was to raid the melon patch of a family with whom we were having a fancied feud at the time. But raiding aside, that childhood memory of Indiana home-grown melons, like that of Indiana home-grown tomatoes, makes it difficult to shop at the modern produce department.

As summer progressed, our cornfield calendar shifted into its mature stage. The stalks would be so tall and heavily loaded with ears as to defy our running down the rows. By this time leaves would be loaded with spent pollen, pumpkins scattered throughout the field were beginning to show splotches of yellowish-orange through the green skin, and overall would hang a vaguely disturbing feeling that school was about to begin.

All too soon early September would find us trooping down our lane and along the dusty road toward Green Hill school. Our route to school was bound on both sides by mature fields of corn which we had watched burst from the ground as tiny seedlings only three and one-half months earlier. As we made these daily walks, we watched the fields change from solid green to streaky shades of green and tan. And soon thereafter would come the day when Daddy would be on the grindstone as we left for school, sharpening a machete-like corn cutter. Then as we returned, along one side of the field, we would find a row of teepee-like corn shocks which had been undisturbed corn stalks in the morning.

Cutting and shocking corn by hand used to be to us children one of those most dramatic and satisfying of farming procedures, perhaps because it was one which young children could only observe. A corn shock was formed of a group of corn stalks ten hills by ten hills square, thus one-hundred hills or three-hundred stalks. A good worker could cut and shock seventy shocks per day, which is about two acres. And so right before our eyes as we trudged to and from school, some of our familiar cornfields were converted by Daddy into picturesque Indian teepee villages. These extended uphill and downhill all over the fields, but always in perfectly geometric comformation and spacing. At the same time that this dramatic landscape transformation was occurring on our farm, it was occurring on neighboring farms, creating this unique autumnal landscape from horizon to horizon. Between and among the shocks of corn would appear the big yellow pumpkins heretofore obscured by the dense cornstalk foliage. It was one of childhood's most picturesque annual dramas, and it is small wonder that the words of James Whitcomb Riley "When the frost is on the punkin and the fodder's in the shock" were so dear to all of us in Indiana.

Soon would come corn-shucking, and from this operation we children were not excused. By mid-October the frost-killed corn left standing on the stalk in uncut fields would be turning brown and sere. On Saturdays we boys would help Daddy "shuck corn," although he could handle more rows himself than the three of us together. Cornhusking, as it was called in other parts of the Midwest, was in those days a skill of such magnitude that local, state and national contests were held, resulting in a national cornhusking championship. Daddy was not a champion, but was pretty good and to us boys a marvel to behold. The technique is to grab an ear with the left hand, rip the shuck off the opposite side of it with a peg or hook strapped in the palm of the right hand, then in the same motion grab the thus bared portion of the ear with the right hand, while the left hand has pulled off the other half of the shuck and slipped to the butt of the ear to provide a fulcrum against which to snap the ear off its stem with the right hand. Daddy could have two perfectly stripped ears in the air at once and be diving at a third before the first one hit the "bangboard" on the far side of the wagon.

The corn we shucked from the stalk and the corn we shucked from the shock all had to be shoveled by hand into one or the other of our two corn cribs, both of which were built in conjunction with hog houses. This newly shucked corn made such a beautiful golden-yellow treasure in the corn cribs and smelled so clean and fresh that it seemed a shame to shovel it each day to the pigs waiting expectantly below. But all this reluctance was forgotten once the pigs were observed receiving a scoop shovel of corn. A pig can consume an ear of dry, hard field corn with the same gusto, efficiency and apparent enjoyment as that with which our own species consumes an ear of green sweet corn. Such a crunching and munching did they make that I would sit there on the overhead crib steps as a child feeding them ear after ear just to listen to them smack their chops and crunch.

There was this same fascination in feeding whole-ear corn to the horses, which we did during the work season. This was one of the jobs for us kids in the summer time—to always have water in the horse tank at noon, and to have placed six ears of corn in each manger box and plenty of hay in each hay manger. Thus when Daddy came in from the field at noon, the horses could go directly to water and feed. Well do I remember these chores, because the last time Daddy gave us three boys a spanking was for failing to pump the noonday water for the horses. By the time we saw him coming up from the barn, in an unusually grim and purposeful stride, it was too late, and we had that

awful childhood feeling of impending doom. But we gave it our best shot. When Daddy entered the pump house, we were all three on the pump handle trying to look sweaty and virtuous as if we had been pumping since dawn. But Daddy was not impressed—and gave each of us a spanking right then and there—a triple header, or more appropriately a triple seater. For several days thereafter we kept the horse tank filled to a depth theretofore unknown except on Thrashing Day.

But back to feeding ears of corn to the horses. Because the grain boxes were built of wood as a part of the manger structure, the wood served as a sounding board for each bite a horse would take from an ear, and for each grain of dry corn crunched between the horse's teeth. The result was a booming "carrump, carrump" followed by such a resonating crunching that the sounds of all four horses lunching at one time will be forever stored in my mind.

For the cows we chopped each ear of corn into three or four pieces, and placed the equivalent of three or four ears of corn in each feed box in front of each milking stanchion. In the fall of the year, when pumpkins were still remaining from the wagon loads we had brought in from the cornfields, we also put chopped pumpkins in the feed boxes for the cows. Then we would open the stable door through which each milk cow would file to her personal stanchion. It was fun to watch the pigs and horses eat their corn-on-the-cob, but nothing compared to observing our Jersey cows consuming the chunks of corn and pumpkin. Jersey cows have naturally sweet and expressive faces anyhow, and the chunks were of such size that the cows could not readily get them between their molars. This resulted in such a lop-sided shifting of jaws, rolling of eyes and lashing of tongues that the view down the row of cow faces was unique, to say the least. Equally memorable to me from my childhood recollection of placing feed in the cow mangers is that meadow-sweet mixed fragrance of cow's breath and sweet clover hay. Too bad it could not be bottled.

It was necessary that we shell the corn for the chickens, and because we children did most of the chicken chores, we were very well acquainted with the shelling operation. In those days there were all sorts of corn shellers, but ours was one of the bigger and better ones. It stood around four and one-half feet high, with ample space under the grain exit to set a bushel basket or five-gallon bucket. It had a feeding hopper large enough to hold almost a bushel of corn ears and a fly wheel which, once revved up, would maintain momentum with very little cranking. (Now that I think about it, this same heavy fly wheel would have whipped a child's arm through the sheller with the same unrelenting speed as an ear of corn, but fortunately this did not happen to us.)

Because we kept from three hundred to a thousand chickens, we put a lot of corn through that sheller, resulting in a large volume of corncobs. But corncobs never were wasted on the farm. In fact the uses of corncobs may have rivaled the uses of corn. Nothing was as handy for starting quick, hot fires in the kitchen range as corncobs. A handful of corncobs plus a dollop of coal oil was the standard fire-starting procedure. Therefore there was always a bucket or basket of corncobs in the woodbox, and a wagon load of them in the corncob bin in the woodhouse.

Corncobs were used also as a staple in smoking our hams and bacon, along with hickory wood. Connoisseurs of home-smoked meat of the time were about equally divided in the use of corncobs or hickory as prime sources of smoke. Corncobs were also the standard cork or plug of the time. The typical water jug carried to the fields at harvest time was the one-gallon, gray and brown stone jug, corked by the ubiquitous corncob. In the interest of sanitation and a better seal, this corncob usually was enfolded in a piece of soft, thick cloth, the equally ubiquitous piece of long underwear. This same combination was found in use everywhere, no matter on what farm or in what field, or whether as a cork for a water jug, a vinegar jug, a cider jug or a kerosene jug. A corncob and a ragged swatch of used longjohns did the job. It was the universal plug.

The corncob had another use in the farm community which, although seldom mentioned, placed it in direct competition with the Sears and Roebuck catalog—the used catalog. In fact among the more outdoor, back-of-the-barn types the corncob had a very loyal, even vocal constituency. The first expression I ever heard in this regard, "takes off all the new and some of the old," came at a time when I was so young that I puzzled over it for years. I have not heard this remark for over sixty-five years, which is probably just as well; although I must admit it does have a certain earthy piquancy. But suffice it to say that some of the better outhouses in our community provided a box of corncobs in addition to a Sears and Roebuck catalog.

As suggested above, very little of the corn plant was wasted. Usually the corn was shucked from the fodder shocks right in the field, after which the fodder was tied in bundles. These bundles were set up again into huge bundle shocks, in order to resist weather until they could be hauled into the barn for cattle feed. Because these bundles of fodder were so conveniently available in the fields at Halloween, teenaged boys found them irresistible for use in Halloween devilment. Blocking lanes and roads was an obvious use. Another was to stuff outhouses—those which could not more conveniently be pushed over.

In the old days, we are told, corn shocks with the ears intact were hauled into the barn for shucking, resulting in what were known as husking bees. We rarely brought any shocks inside for shucking, but I remember once when we did so, even doing some of the shucking by lantern light. It is easy to see how this practice could have been turned into a popular social occasion, particularly among teenagers and the generally young-at-heart.

Much has been said above concerning table use of green corn but nothing about culinary use of dry corn. So let me say that we grew our own popcorn, dried and shelled it ourselves and had popcorn and apples almost every night in winter. In fact, it is still difficult for me to read in the evening without one or both at hand. Tom Thumb was one of our favorite popcorn varieties then, and is still available in seed catalogs today.

We also had, in spite of my most fervid childhood protests, home-made hominy. Mother seemed to think hominy was good or else good for us, because she was always soaking freshly shelled corn in lye water to get the hulls off, then washing and boiling the result into hominy. To this day I can see no point in this abominable product, although I remember it well. On the credit side, we often had corn meal pancakes, which I still remember fondly, and even more often we had corn meal mush. This was really good eaten with melting butter on top, plus brown sugar and milk. And best of all was the left-over mush, sliced cold the next day and then fried in a skillet to a waxy, crusty brown and served for breakfast with fresh sorghum molasses!

Truly it could be said that on the Indiana farm of my childhood, corn was the staff of life.

CHAPTER VII

THRASHING DAY

In childhood memories of Indiana farm life of the 1920s, threshing day is unequalled for sheer intensity and volume of action and also for volume of good food. No one of the time ever would have said "threshing." It was always "thrashing." It was carried on within a "thrashing ring" and the actual grain-separator was the "thrashing machine."

Our threshing ring of the time included a group of ten or twelve neighboring farmers who had formed together in joint ownership of a grain separator. This machine was pulled from farm to farm and set up to thresh out the grain from wagon loads of bundles hauled to it from the fields. It was the stationary equivalent of the present day self-propelled combine and required a large crew for operation, because the straw had to be brought to the machine instead of machine going to the standing grain.

Our threshing crew of farm neighbors included six bundle wagons (each with driver and team of horses), two grain wagons, four "pitchers" (men with pitchfork), the tractor and threshing machine operator—a total crew of fourteen men. Farms in our threshing ring included those owned by: Fred Kaderly (owner of the tractor), Ollie Ashley, Dewey Smith, the Rudy sisters, Tom Corle, Harry Lyons, Forest Greaf, Clarence Strauss, Denny Flint,Charlie Shreeve, Everett Robson, and our farm, of course. These farms formed a rough "ring" on both sides of the road surrounding a square mile of land, and ranged in size from forty to two-hundred acres.

In early August, after all wheat, rye, barley and

oats had been cut by individually-owned binders (and shocked by sweating, itching and complaining farm children) the president of the threshing ring would call an evening meeting. At this meeting names were put in a hat and drawn to determine who would supply the pitcher and who would supply teams and wagons, and on whose farm the operation would commence.

In retrospect, it must have been an anxious time for farm wives, not having much advance notice on what day they would have to cook up a noon meal for fourteen hungry "thrashers." But it always seemed to work out quite well. Those dinners for threshers were well known to be the biggest of the year, so much so that whenever any housewife of the time wished to emphasize having cooked a big batch of something, she would say "enough for thrashers."

Fortunately, the time of year conformed nicely to a time of abundance in the garden, orchard and chicken lot. On the afternoon of the day before threshers were expected, we kids would be enlisted by Mother to help catch some chickens. This we did quite willingly, not only for an opportunity to run but also in anticipation of the end result. In those days, frying chickens were real frying chickens. They were firm, full-flavored, range-running young roosters, not the flacid, battery-fed plastic chickens of today. To catch them required a bit of running, but after creating great squawkings and flappings of wings, we soon would be carrying six or eight now quiet and subdued young roosters by the feet, to a rendezvous with the chopping block.

Now that I look back, it is difficult to believe that we kids suffered no pangs of pity for these beautiful birds. It seems almost odd also that so kind and gentle a person as Mother could calmly and efficiently decapitate these roosters and leave them flapping out their life's blood on the wood chips behind the woodhouse. But it was all in the day's work then, and soon we would be picking the feathers off the scalded birds, while chattering away about "thrashing dinner." To this day the not unpleasant smell of wet, scalded chicken feathers comes back to me as if I were there sixty-five years ago.

The next morning Mother would have volunteer culinary help in the kitchen in the form of one of our aunts or a neighbor, and there would be a great bustle of rolling pins and biscuit cutters, peeling of potatoes and apples and snapping of green beans. There was not much time for children, but there was an air of everything's being done with cheerful efficiency, regardless of what must have been considerable stress. We were soon to go outside, because entering the lane was the thrashing machine! On it came, this huge galvanized monster, with its long neck folded back over its body, and being pulled by Fred Kaderly's Hart Parr tractor, the biggest tractor in our neighborhood. Soon it was guided through the gate and into the stable yard behind the barn, where last year's strawstack was but a memory. After consultation with Daddy, the crew would tow the machine into position, with its neck (blower) pointing toward the site of last year's strawstack. Then Fred and his oldest boy, Elmer, would unroll a huge belt, reaching about fifty feet from the drive shaft of the machine to the power shaft of the tractor. They would slip it onto both drive heads and back the tractor just enough to tighten the belt. Next they would mark the position of the tractor wheel, move the the tractor a few feet, dig a depression in the ground to receive the wheel, move the tractor back with the wheel in the hole and the belt tight. This maneuver we watched with great interest, as if we were going to have to do it ourselves some day.

Fred Kaderly was a bit of a study himself, a short-legged and short-bodied man whose long arms and humped shoulders gave him a troglodytic look. This look was intensified by the simian agility with which he clambered over, under, and inside the monstrous machine with a grease gun, in preparation for the bundle wagons about to arrive. With impressive mechanical precision the long, telescoped blower was cranked from its rest atop the machine and swung around over the strawstack site. Elevated to a convenient angle, its movable steel upper lip was then lowered to shoot the straw on the exact spot for the beginning of the stack. The thrashing machine was now ready to thrash. As if aware of its impatience, Fred Kaderly would engage the drive shaft clutch, and the entire thing would roar into thundering, clanking and vibrating action, the big triangular teeth at the upper end of the bundle conveyor chomping up and down like dragon's teeth in the mouth of a hungry dragon.

By this time the first two wagonloads of our wheat bundles would have been pulled into position alongside the clattering bundle conveyer. Inside the bundle conveyor was an endless procession of slats relaying the bundles relentlessly into the cavernous mouth of the thrashing machine. The wagon on one side of the bundle chute may have been driven by Irv Eley, with his perfectly matched and beautifully harnessed bay mules, Jack and Duke. Irv could form one of the neatest bundle loads in the neighborhood, the butt of every sheaf exactly even with its neighbor, so that the load looked as if it had been squared up by huge shears after being loaded.

As if by contrast, on the other side of the conveyer could be the wagon of Denny Flint, with a lopsided "jag" of bundles drawn by a painfully thin and bony, gray speckled team, harnessed in little more than horse collars and chain tugs. Denny owned the smallest and least fertile farm in the ring and was as poor and stingy as a Dickens character. For example, when hunting rabbits with a .22, Denny, if he found one sitting in its grass form, would move around behind it, remove his shoes, then slip up and grab it with his hands to save the cost of a .22 bullet, about three-eighths of a cent. And on his place Denny ran a painfully tight ship. Therefore his poor horses had no collar pads and had great collar sores on their shoulders all summer long.

On signal from Fred Kaderly, Irv and Denny would begin tossing bundles onto the conveyer, heads forward, each alternating with the other to keep an even flow of grain going into the separator. As each wagon driver completed unloading his wagon, he would drive back to the field, where he would be approached by a "pitcher" who would commence pitching bundles to him one at a time from a shock of grain. A good pitcher could make it easy for the loader, by presenting each bundle with the proper orientation so that it would not need be turned by the loader.

Our wagon beds were about eight feet wide and twelve feet long, with a "standard" at both ends eight feet high. A good load was built by laying the first row of bundles tightly side by side on the far side of the wagon, with the butts extending one foot beyond the wagon bed. The next row of bundles would be laid the same way on the near side of the wagon bed. This would leave the middle of the wagon bed still bare, and the next row of bundles would be laid down this middle area, with each sheaf overlapping the heads of the first row about halfway, thus tying each preceding sheaf in place. The sheaves in the middle row were alternated with regard to direction of head and butt, to keep the load composition exactly uniform. As each layer was completed, the loader would go to the point of beginning and build the next layer. The best loader could build a load exactly rectangular and eight or nine feet high, and took pride in doing so.

Meanwhile back at the barnyard we children would still be watching, fascinated by the unfolding spectacle. Harry Lyons and Charley Shreeve might have replaced Irv and Denny at the bundle chute. Harry would be riding a load of bundles rivalling that of Irv Eley and driving a pair of sturdy bays, Dick and Frank. In the midst of all the fire hazard of chaff and straw, he probably would still have his pipe in his mouth and his straw hat at a jaunty angle. Charley Shreeve, who had a wheezy, yet high-pitched voice like that old character actor, Andy Devine, would be screeching at his ever restless team like a soul demented. Fortunately for us spectators, his horses paid so little attention that his entire stay at the bundle chute was one continuous comedy act.

By this time the wheat, barley, rye or oats would be spewing out of the elevator spout in such volume that the grain wagon would be the site of much activity, in which we could be helpful. The procedure was to slip the open mouth of an empty grain sack under the spout, as soon as the preceding one was filled so that very little grain would be spilled into the wagon bed. We children were good at that and good at making sure the empty sacks were at hand. In those days each farmer had as many as a hundred, standard two-bushel capacity, tightly woven grain sacks, a real necessity at threshing time. Each of these sacks when filled with wheat weighed one-hundred-twenty pounds. Boys were considered to be reasonably good "hands" when they could flip one of these filled and tied sacks on one shoulder and climb a ladder to the wheat bin to empty the sack and repeat the procedure for hours.

But to us children the lure of the grain bins was for play, not work. What fun it was to position ourselves near the dumping point of the sacks of wheat until so nearly buried that wriggling to the surface was a real effort. We called it "quicksand" and waded in it until the bins became filled so close to the ceiling that we could no longer stand up.

Along toward noon we would have been saturated by events in the barnyard and would return to the house for a change of scene. By this time the kitchen and summer kitchen were filled with cooling apple pies and pitchers of lemonade mixings, and the dining room table was being extended to full length. By putting in all our finished table boards and some plain boards, the table could seat six on each side and two at each end—just right for thrashers.

When given the word from the kitchen, someone shut down the separator, and in the strange silence the teamsters quietly went about watering and feeding their horses, while the other hands began to drift toward the house. Here we children had helped set out all available wash pans on up-ended egg crates and old chairs under the maple trees outside the house. For washing, we had provided buckets of well water, with dippers—the same for drinking. We hung towels on the clothesline and even brought out "the comb" from its oilcloth pocket under the looking glass on the kitchen wall. Then we lined up just to watch.

It was interesting to see the dust-caked men each roll his used cud of tobacco into a cupped hand, then look around for a place to throw it out of sight. And with clinical interest we watched bald heads emerge from under dusty, sweat-stained hats. We noticed that Fred Kaderly first soaped his hands and arms, then his face and right up over his bald head, and after rinsing in the washpan, poured a dipper of water right over his head, scrubbing it off with the other hand! So that's how bald men washed, we thought, making mental notes. All of the men were caked with sweat and chaff when they came up, and when they had finished washing, and combing their hair (with the family comb) they sat down in the shade looking very pleased with themselves.

When all were washed up, Daddy would lead them toward the dining room door, where they would sidle in as if walking on eggs and silently get arranged around the table. Then Daddy would say a short grace, thanking the Lord for "this good food and these good neighbors," following which everyone would relax and start exchanging conversation and food. There would be big platters of fried chicken, lots of mashed potatoes and gravy, dozens of hot baking powder biscuits, green beans, creamed corn, sliced tomatoes, pickled beets and cucumber pickles, strawberry jam, and lemonade with ice in the pitchers. For dessert would be open apple pie, for which Mother was locally famous.

All four of us children would stand around watching and listening to every word. There was the usual ribbing of the fast eaters and the big eaters—that somebody could "load more on his plate than on his wagon." There was talk of quality of grain and bushels per acre and acres yet to do—of past thrashings and upset loads and runaway horses. Dinner finished, the men would head for the door with much self-conscious comment to Mother and our aunt about how good the food was, then out to the shade of the maple trees for a smoke or a fresh "chaw" of Mail Pouch, Beech

Nut, Red Man or Bagpipe.

As soon as the table could be cleared, we children and "the cooks" could sit at one end of the extended table and have our own thrashing dinner. Everything tasted twice as good for having had to wait until second table. And there was lots to talk about—who said what, and who did this or that. And we had much of our own stuff to tell— how much fun it was to help with the wheat in the bins and how big the strawstack was getting to be. Mother must have been very much relieved to have seen everything come off so well and to have successfully "cooked for thrashers" again.

After dinner we would slip out to the barnyard again, by now a bit more selective in what we did, spending more time in the shade and out of the flying dust and chaff. By late afternoon the last load of bundles would be alongside the conveyer and we would watch the last one being whisked up the conveyer and under the flashing teeth of the chomping jaws, to disappear into the stomach of the galvanized dragon. We would see the last teamster pull away from the conveyer, jump off his wagon and conscientiously fork any dropped bundles and loose straw into the conveyer then climb back on his wagon and pull away to the neighboring farm of Irv Eley, next in the "ring."

Shortly thereafter Fred Kaderly would shut down the clattering machine, and in the deafening silence immediately crank the now fully extended blower back to its telescoped position around over the top of the separator and lower it to its resting place on the back of the machine, exactly as a goose lays its neck over its back when it prepares to sleep. Soon Fred and Elmer would have the drive belt rolled up on the drive head and the tractor hitched to the front of the separator. Then the huge machine would

start on its way around the strawstack, through the gate and up the lane to its next job.

Once more we kids were alone in our barnyard. But what had become of it? What once had been a spacious loafing area for cows, horse and sheep had all but disappeared under a huge conical mountain of golden straw, towering to the sky. So high was its peak, and so wide its base, that we hardly knew where to start to climb it. But climb it we did, although the straw was so loose that we almost disappeared on our way up. Then remembering that Daddy had told us not to play on the strawstack until it had settled, we rolled down to the bottom, where we stood back marveling at our tracks to the top. Had we really been all the way up there?

Another Thrashing Day was over.

This childhood memory depicts a true but ephemerally short phase of life on Midwestern farms of America. Although we children believed that this is the way life on the family farm always had been and always would be, the reader should be reminded that the threshing machine period lasted only fifty years. It commenced with the steam engine driven machine on the big grain farms of Iowa, Kansas and the Dakotas back around 1890 and ended abruptly at the advent of World War II in 1941. Our own threshing ring broke up in 1941.

I feel very fortunate to have experienced this time of neighborly cooperation in grain harvest. To enter the threshing ring as a full fledged "hand" was a rite of passage into manhood for every farm boy of the time. Each of my two brothers and I in turn passed into this rite on reaching age fifteen. It was excellent training for life, as well as being interesting and enjoyable at the time. Too bad there is absolutely no counterpart in the life of all boys in America today.

CHAPTER VIII

APPLE BUTTER AND SORGHUM MOLASSES

Although Mother used to "put up" various jams and jellies, the staple sweeteners and sandwich fillers on the farm of my childhood were honey, sorghum molasses and apple butter. Because honey was provided to us by Uncle Ott, who kept fifteen or twenty stands of bees in our orchard, I will tell here only of apple butter and molasses-making.

It was necessary that apple butter day immediately follow cider-making, because an important ingredient in old fashioned apple butter was fresh apple cider, boiled down to a sweet, rich apple syrup. This boiling was commenced early in the morning of apple butter day, immediately on arrival of the "apple peelers," in the form of two or more of our aunts, with or without uncles.

Our Aunt Lulu would always come and would bring along the much prized apple butter kettle, a huge gleaming copper monster of even greater capacity than the iron butchering kettles. It was owned by our grandfather (whom we kids were taught to call "Granpap"), and whom our father and all his siblings called "Pap." Evidently Granpap prized this kettle quite highly, as we were warned by Daddy to "stay away from it." Looking back, it seems to me that this kettle could be called a family heirloom, and I wonder where it is today.

At any rate this kettle was the centerpiece for apple butter day, when it was hung in impressive splendor on the butchering kettle pole. Fresh cider from the cider bar-

rel was siphoned into buckets and poured into the apple butter kettle, under which an ample fire was now crackling. All of this was well attended by us children, and each of us "helped" in siphoning the cider into the buckets and ourselves. Even as I write I can taste the cold, fresh cider from the siphon, smell the wood smoke, hear the chatter of Aunt Lulu, (pronounced Lulie) and Aunt Pearl (read Pearlie) and see the cats assembling in hope that this might be butchering day.

Inside the house the "womenfolks" would have the apple peelers (also courtesy of Granpap) clamped to the table or clamped to a board across two chairs, and would be engaged in converting baskets and buckets of Winter Maidenblush apples into "apple schnitz," meaning peeled, quartered and cored apples. All of this activity and lots of things cooking on the kitchen range created a steamy, noisy atmosphere in the kitchen. This was the nearest thing to a party that ever occurred at our house.

Although the copper kettle was the center of interest outside, the apple peeler was the center of interest inside. To us kids, unexposed to mechanical devices, this apple peeler was the ultimate marvel. (The reader should keep in mind that an automobile was still referred to by its owner as "The Machine." "We drove The Machine," or "Go warm up The Machine.") Therefore we all had to take turns at the apple peeler, fascinated by the way the blade could adjust itself to the stem end of the apple as well as the blossom end, and by the unbroken length of the golden ribbon of peel which could be produced in seconds.

By the time the apples had been peeled and cored, the cider would have boiled down by half, providing room in the kettle for addition of buckets of apple schnitz. As the apples and cider continued cooking over the open fire, the stirring paddle would come into play. This was not just a simple paddle, as was used in stirring lard, but was a device made especially for use in the big, flat-bottomed apple butter kettle. Essentially it consisted of a long wooden handle, to which was attached at right angle a thick maple slab at least a foot square, with one-inch holes through it. Because the handle was so long and the paddle so heavy, it was suspended over the kettle by a special frame, supporting the paddle while permitting it to contact the entire kettle area.

From this it can be seen that stirring apple butter was not a task to be taken lightly. In fact, it appears that making good apple butter was due mainly to the stirring and the quality of the apples, in that no ingredients were used except apples and cider. Thus the sweetening came from concentration of the fructose contained in the cider and apple schnitz. This concentration process also heightened the apple flavor of the resulting product.

As the process neared the finished stage, various members of the crew were called upon to try samples from the tasting dish on a nearby chopping block, where samples were constantly cooling. The important factor in timing was to remove the butter from the fire at a stage when flavor was at its height and before color had unduly darkened. The ideal product was light brown, creamy thick but not stiff, and had a full, rich apple flavor with no trace of burn or scorch.

When a consensus was reached, two adults at each end of the pole lifted the kettle from over the fire and set it on the ground for convenient access. From there it was ladled into one gallon stone crocks and sealed with melted

paraffin. An average batch yielded at least twenty-five or thirty gallons of apple butter. This was divided up among the participants in some manner seemingly pre-arranged, or perhaps just tacitly in effect. At any rate, there was apple butter for all, for at least another year, and thoughts could be turned to other things, which to us kids meant mostly good things to eat.

One of these good things was sorghum molasses, and the time for sorghum-pressing came about the same time as cider-pressing and apple-butter-making. Actual growing of the sorghum-cane required several months, of course, but was not a very complex procedure.

The sorghum grain was seeded in rows like corn rows and at about the same time. The stalks of sorghum resembled corn stalks, but unlike our corn crop, the sorghum rows could only be cultivated in one direction. It therefore required hoeing and weeding by hand, as did potatoes, beans and other major food crops, which we called "truck," and which were grown in the "truck patch."

And so it was that our several long rows of sorghum grew all summer in the truck patch and were tended along with navy beans, potatoes and kraut cabbage. By early fall, and prior to a killing frost, came the time to "strip the cane." This was one of our favorite jobs and was done either with plaster lath, broom handles, or corn cutters. Sticks were more fun than corn cutters, because you could simply lash out and in one satisfyingly noisy blow, strip every leaf off one side of a six-foot cane stalk and with a second blow leave it standing there like a bamboo fishing pole, completely naked and leafless. Seldom can a farm boy slash out around himself with such abandon without later being punished for breaking something. So stripping cane was a great tension reliever, psychologically thera-peutic for us farm children, although we probably were not under any great tensions.

When stripping was completed, we cut the naked stalks near the ground with corn cutters and laid them in neat piles alongside the cane row. Here our cane would remain until such time as it would be convenient for Daddy to haul it to the sorghum mill. This time lag meant that whenever we needed something sweet to chew on, we could pick up a stalk of cane from one of the piles, cut it into convenient lengths, peel off the tough skin and chew the pulp.

We did not accompany the cane to the cane mill in the big wagon, mainly because the mill did not press the cane immediately on arrival, but generally a few days later. However, we were always on hand when several five-gal-lon cans (the same as the lard cans) were brought home, containing our "new molasses." Like new apple butter, new molasses had that fresh, mild flavor which was ea-gerly awaited by us consumers, and we would immedi-ately eat some with spoons, directly from the can. In all fairness, however, I must admit that as time passed the flavor and color of both apple butter and sorghum (and lard) deteriorated somewhat under storage in unprotected cans and stone crockery.

For school lunches, carried in one-gallon Karo syrup buckets, the big three sandwich fillers as mentioned ear-lier were molasses, apple butter, and honey, each accom-panied by butter, of course. I can remember that the fall school season started off well, with fresh, light brown apple butter or molasses sandwiches, but by spring the apple butter was almost black and somewhat tart and the molasses black and strong-flavored. Honey was good the season long, but honey tended to soak through the homemade bread so that by lunch time, the bread would be as sticky on the outside as on the inside. The same was true of molasses, of course. However, I used to sit with one classmate not really from a farm family, who had nothing in his sandwiches month after month except lard, with pepper sprinkled on it. That always renewed my appreciation of our homemade apple butter and sorghum molasses.

CHAPTER IX

OF NUTS AND SQUIRRELS

There must be a bit of the squirrel in all of us—something in our genetic history urging us to gather and store things. This primal urge appears to be particularly strong in the fall of the year, with the coming of those cool, crisp days following the first hard frost.

This autumnal motivation is stronger in some individuals than others. Some manage to fend it off merely by picking up a bag of Fritos and settling down to watch a football game on TV. Others, more affluent, evade it by digging out travel brochures and planning a trip to Hawaii or by buying and storing CD's or treasury bills. Others, even more affluent, manage to subvert it completely by cashing in their treasury bills and moving residence to Hawaii, where there are no cool, crisp days and no hard frosts.

In my own case there must have been an ancestral epoch when my family and the squirrel family shared common cells of the cambium layer of the family tree. When fall comes for me, it's gather and store or die. Each nut, apple, potato, tomato, pepper or onion is like a gleaming treasure to be gathered, picked, dug, plucked or pulled and squirreled away for the winter.

This instinctive urge may account for the fact that one of my earliest recollections of childhood on our Indiana farm is of gathering walnuts and hickory nuts in autumn. Always looking for a chance to escape to the woods anyhow, the four of us saw nut-gathering as custom-made. Even today the smell of a black walnut husk brings it all surging back in vivid nostalgia—the cool, fragrant air, the riot of fall colors, the sharp, indignant chatter of startled squirrels, and the subsequent rustle of leaves as the furry animals bounded across the forest floor, away from fancied harm.

One special memory is of the time when we four, still very small, decided that the really efficient and painless way to transport our treasure from the woods to the house would be to use the "little wagon." We called it the "little wagon" in order not to confuse it with the "big wagon," as both wagons were household words in those days. Our sturdy but much battered little wooden wagon was fairly easy to pull or push on the smooth pathways and lanes around the house. However, we had not calculated some of the negative effects of rough ground, mud, and uphill travel when planning our four-wheel transport venture.

So off we went, the four of us, the little wagon bouncing along behind us at the end of a rope tied to the tongue. In no time at all we had made our way down the big hill to the creek, which we were pleased to find presented no problem for the wagon, then up the hill and into the woods. Here we crossed a small, dry, branch creek, then on to our favorite walnut tree, very pleased with ourselves. It was a perfect day, and we had the perfect plan for it.

There was a trace of the overnight frost on the grass beneath our walnut tree. In the still air the big palmate walnut leaves were silently separating from their parent twigs and floating to the ground in a green and gold shower. Occasionally a fat, heavy walnut, loosened by the same frost, separated from its stem and hit the ground with a solid thump. We had timed our mechanized harvest to the minute!

The first club we threw into the tree proved our timing. Big, fat walnuts dropped by the dozens, the higher ones dislodging lower ones on the way down—the entire accumulation hitting the ground with a muffled roar. We had struck it rich—the Mother Lode of walnuts! Soon we had the ground so heavily littered that we were stumbling over the round, pungent fruit of the tree, and it was time to start picking the walnuts. There is something satisfying about thumping those big, rough nuts into a bucket and dumping the bucket into a bag, and soon we had our two bags filled and tied. On finding the bags too heavy to lift, we were pleased to learn that we could bring the wagon alongside, then tip the bag across the wagon—and so managed to load the two bags side by side.

The beginning of our return trip was downhill to the little branch creek, and thus not too difficult. Crossing this branch was a test of our muscles (and our sibling relationships), but we managed to hold things together and continued down to the main creek. After a brief consultation which, like most committee meetings produced nothing new, we decided to charge ahead at full speed with two pulling and two pushing. However, in the middle of the creek, which was little more than a trickle over a muck of horse and cow tracks, the wagon wheels bogged down in the mud. This I remember as one of life's very first crises.

Somehow or other we completed the crossing, because I well remember that sibling tension surfaced again in our labors up the big hill. By this time the frost was long gone and the sun was high, making us overdressed for our struggle on the sunny south slope, separating our house from the creek. I do not remember exactly how we accomplished the ascent, but the fact that the effort sticks in my

memory at all, after sixty-seven years is evidence that it was not easy. Despite all our puffing and sweating on that hillside, it never occurred to us to unload one sack, then return for it. The important thing is that we did manage to get our treasure home, and spread out under the big Maple back of the house to age a bit before hulling.

Hulling walnuts was one of those sedentary and companionable family activities like shelling peas, except much more fun. Probably it was more fun because our parents usually dropped out early, leaving it up to us children to pursue our own special techniques. The most satisfying of these was to sit down with a heavy board between outstretched legs, place a fat, juicy walnut on the board and swat it with a flat, heavy paddle. This resulted in an effective popping of the nut from the husk, as well as an effective splatter of juicy brown walnut stain all over nearby siblings. By the end of the walnut-hulling season we looked like Indian children wearing brown denim bib overalls.

In gathering hickory nuts, we paid more attention to quality than we did in gathering walnuts. In our woods the hickory trees were more numerous than were the walnut trees, and also varied much more in nut quality. The nuts from some were thin-shelled and sweet, while others, although thin-shelled, were flavorless. Some trees produced very large nuts, and usually these were thick-shelled. Some large hickory nuts released their meats (which we knew only as "goodies") easily on cracking, while others confined their meat in such a way as to defy access to much more than crumbs, dug out with a hairpin. So we soon learned and remembered which trees yielded nuts with the best qualities of their particular type.

It was necessary to club hickory nuts to the ground at a less mature stage than walnuts, for, if we left them to ripen, Fox, Grey and Red Squirrels would beat us to the harvest. I do remember one way we could "get even" with the squirrels, however. It so happened that in the middle of the woods stood a hollow beech tree—a veritable artist's conception of a hollow tree, with a big perfectly round hole about three feet off the ground. Squirrels turned this tree into an annual storehouse, jamming it so full of nuts that some rolled out on the ground. We could count on this storehouse as an easy means to augment our own supply of nuts. In thinking back, I seem to remember that we left about half of this chock-full-of-nuts store for the squirrels, but I am not sure that pure altruism was at work here. It may be that we could reach down only about halfway to the bottom of the store. I do hope this was not the only reason we shared the cache.

So enough about nut-gathering, how about nut-eating? Upstairs in our farmhouse was an unfinished room with a brick chimney running through it to the roof. Up here the hulled nuts were spread to dry; and up here we spent countless winter hours, backs against the warm chimney, old flat irons between our knees, passing the claw hammer around, pigging out (or squirreling out) on the rewards of our autumn labors. We didn't even worry about cleaning up the empty shells, which by spring covered the floor in a thick, brown mulch. Our bushy-tailed, furbearing little friends in their hollow trees down in the wintry woods had nothing on us. We had our own hollow tree!

CHAPTER X

APPLE CIDER

In a one to ten scale of gustatory memories of my childhood on an Indiana farm, cider-making day gets a nine, right below butchering day. Unfortunately, the taste of freshly pressed cider from a proper blend of apples can be only a memory in America of today. Apple juice available in super market grocery departments is only a pallid ghost of the real thing, for at least two reasons. One of these is that it is made from one, two or three of the common commercial apple varieties, probably Red Delicious, Yellow Delicious, Rome Beauty or Jonathan. All of these are too bland for cider. Pasteurization for shelf life is another cause of blandness in available ciders of today. Good cider can be made only from a blend of several different varieties of apples ranging from sweet to acid and including aromatic and tangy types—and must remain unpasteurized.

It is difficult for me to separate cider-making from apple-picking, as the two used to come around the first week of November, and are interrelated in fond memories of our orchard. It is also difficult for me to picture life on our family farm without our beloved orchard. As children, we used to spend half our free time there. It was the next best thing to being in the woods. What else could provide that glorious rush of springtime color, with acres of white and pink blossoms against clear blue sky in May, loading the air with a fragrance that perfumed our childhood world?

What else could provide such a variety of arboreal "jungle gyms" where we played in the cool shade on a hot summer day? What else could provide such easy availability of wonderful munching, from the first Yellow Transparents of early July to those crisp and zesty York Imperials, still to be kicked out of the grass in unfrozen perfection, as late as December?

It is hard to say whether apple-picking was something which simply needed to be done before cider-pressing, or whether cider-pressing was just an aftermath of apple-picking. Both were important to us, and both were fun to do, although apple-picking involved considerable physical exertion. I can remember well the bustle of assembling the dozens of baskets, buckets, burlap feed sacks, ladders, and the entire family, as apple-picking was a family activity in every sense of the word. We usually started with the two big trees of Winesaps, which were wonderful apples, so crisp and juicy that juice would actually squirt out of your mouth when you bit into them. This we did with abandon, dropping some of the apples on the ground after one bite, knowing that they would be picked up for cider and thus not wasted.

From the Winesap trees, we proceeded through the big, waxy, aromatic Winter Maidenblush, and that most flavorful of all apples, the Baldwin. Last to be picked was a late ripening, lop-sided variety known as York Imperials. We picked bushels and bushels and bushels of apples, most of which we carried to the cellar. Here they were stored in the big apple bin and in barrels and sacks for winter use. The resulting aroma in the cellar was almost overwhelming the first few days and lasted for months. A few baskets were left in the garage for casual eating, and many bags and baskets were simply set in the woodhouse, in preparation for apple butter day.

Although we picked lots of apples, we left even more on the trees to be shaken to the ground for cider. Some varieties we had hardly picked at all, such as Ben Davis and Gano, good storage and cider apples, but not comparable to our favorites for eating "out of hand," and so a day or two after apple-picking came the gathering of the cider apples.

Because this could be a somewhat unrestrained activity, and because the end result was such alluring bait, it was not regarded by us kids as "work." In fact, it was fun to climb into the trees and send the apples thumping to the ground by violently shaking the branches. Daddy was particularly impressive to us kids in apple-shaking. He was very strong, and a fearless climber, and I still can hear the rolling thunder of apples which he brought down from an unpicked Ben Davis tree, and see the tumbling cascade of red-striped rivers they made as they rolled down the slope.

Once the apples were all on the ground, we hurried to collect them in baskets and buckets and dump them into burlap feed sacks, which were tightly tied and left standing under the trees. When we were finished, it was strange to see the transformation which had taken place in our orchard within a week's time. Where once had been loads of red and yellow fruit straining the tree limbs to the ground, was now dozens of standing burlap bags. It was as if a congregation of squat, lumpy druids had sprung from the ground and were standing around under the trees dressed in faded burlap, about to begin some sort of nether-world ritual.

Usually within a day or two of bagging the apples, we would hitch Molly and Maud to the big wagon and drive it through the orchard, picking up the bags of apples and setting them solidly, row after row, in the grain bed. These, together with two fifty-gallon barrels, would almost fill the wagon, and off we would go to the cider press about three miles away. We children really didn't learn much about the function of the cider press, as we were always down below the press at a spigot, waiting for the cider to come out.

In retrospect, it seems that we did help unload and dump the bags of apples into a bin from which they flowed by gravity down a chute and into a grinder, and thence into the pressing box, lined with heavy matting. I remember the heavy matting's being folded over each big batch of ground apples, but apparently the instant the squeezing started, my only interest was at the outlet of the holding tank. Here the owner, Dan Baldauf, had thoughtfully provided a hand-operated spigot, flanked by assorted tin cups and jelly glasses. There were even some stools on which to sit while drinking the fresh, foaming fluid from the press. To my way of thinking at the time, nothing more on earth or in heaven could ever be needed!

The actual pressing didn't take long, and soon we were on our triumphant return trip. On reaching home we would carefully roll one of the two barrels down the wagon endgate to the ground near the woodhouse for apple butter and unload the other in the shade of the big cottonwood tree by the old wooden horse trough. Here it would lie for months blocked up on its side. Because it was not immediately provided with a spigot (probably to avoid being drained within days) we would contrive all sorts of withdrawal instruments to satisfy our unquenchable cider thirst. Sweet clover stalks from the horse mangers were good, providing a large volume as well as an intrinsic sweet flavor. But even better was a piece of quarter-inch copper tubing, and best of all a piece of quarter-inch rubber tubing, probably from a tire pump. At any given time, most of these pieces of equipment could be found side by side at the barrel site, and in fact the sweet clover straws tended to grow in number and in length as the cider level receded.

We continued to frequent the cider barrels as the sweet liquid of the first day began to move slowly into its fermentation cycle. By the fifth day the cider was at its peak of flavor—still with full sweetness, but with an added tongue-tickling effect of carbonation. From then on it was a matter of drinking as fast as possible through November, even into the freezing cold of December, when ice need be broken inside the barrel to tap the enclosed liquid. It probably was here that the copper tubing came into play. Eventually, the sweet cider would be on its way to "hard" cider, too flat and tasteless to appeal to children. What was not consumed as sweet cider would be inoculated with "mother" from a vinegar jug and would become our new supply of vinegar. But long before that time we children would already be looking forward to next year's fresh cider-making.

CHAPTER XI

THANKSGIVING DAY

If one holiday stands out in my childhood memories above all others it is Thanksgiving Day—even above Christmas and Fourth of July. And memory tells me quite clearly the reasons for this high priority. Thanksgiving meant rabbit hunting and also a "visit" to our farm by our favorite relatives, Uncle Ott, Aunt Pearlie, Roger and Lois.

It could be argued, I suppose, that the human species today has no instinctive urge to hunt and kill in order to eat, but I disagree. In my opinion three million years of hunter-gatherer history remains strong in all of us, until we are taught not to hunt and gather in our modern cultures and societies. One of my very earliest memories is of a time when I was sick in bed and Daddy came in from hunting with a rabbit tail, which he gave to me to cheer me up. The smell of cold, fresh outdoor air on his clothes, and the rich, furry smell of that ball of fluff, which accounts for the name "cottontail," took me into another world. And when Mother promised me the best piece of rabbit for dinner, I was virtually cured on the spot. It is probable that my account of Thanksgiving Day to follow may seem to dwell insensitively on hunting and killing of rabbits, but that's the way it was.

Uncle Ott and Aunt Pearlie were my mother and father's brother and sister, respectively. Therefore, it was natural that they were our most frequent and favorite adult visitors, and that our double cousin, Roger, was our favorite peer relative.

We didn't have turkeys on our farm, but by Thanks-

giving time our Rhode Island Red or Plymouth Rock roosters were almost as big and fat as turkeys, although still reasonably young. So the big decision for Mother was whether to have roast chicken with dressing or to have stewed chicken and noodles. If it were to be the latter, she would roll out the noodle sheets the night before and drape them on newspapers over the backs of the kitchen chairs to stiffen up an hour or so before she rolled and shaved them into paper-thin noodles. An occasion like Thanksgiving would be about a three-chair noodle batch, and so we kids would go to bed with this visual assurance that the big day was at hand.

Because Uncle Ott was an avid small game hunter, we could depend on seeing his Model T Ford turn into our lane about nine o'clock on Thanksgiving morning. By this time our milking would have been done, the milk run through the DeLaval cream separator, and Daddy would have killed and plucked a seven or eight-pound rooster for Mother as his contribution to fixing dinner. As soon as our guests were inside the door, my two brothers and Roger and I were audibly fidgeting to go rabbit hunting. So Uncle Ott would put on his brown canvas hunting coat, and we would put on our blue denim work "blouses," and be at the door.

Seeing himself the laggard, Daddy would take his old wire-barrelled, full-choke, single-shot twelve gauge from behind the kitchen door and we were off. As soon as our dog Fritz heard the metallic snap of an extractor lever of a shotgun, he would abandon his bed in the woodhouse and dance around us like a puppy. Rabbit-chasing was his own favorite, although futile, pursuit. He was a fox terrier and too short-legged to overtake a healthy rabbit, but never gave up trying; and he had learned that

Thanksgiving Day brought shotguns and that guns skewed the odds strongly in his favor.

Uncle Ott would have his shotgun out of the car by this time, and the click of shells being shoved into pockets and the snap of breech closures was music to our ears as were these same hunting sounds to Fritz. When the guns of the adults were loaded, we all headed immediately for the nearest rabbit cover, usually a pasture or a stubble field. I can feel it now, the cool, invigorating air of late November, laden with autumnal smells of maturing corn fodder and moldering leaves and grass underfoot. I can catch the faint pervasive hint of woodsmoke from kitchen ranges, engaged all over the neighborhood in Thanksgiving cookery.

By this time we were spread out on line, two of us kids between the two adults and one at both outside ends, so that any rabbits flushed would be within range of one gun or the other. Just as tension would begin to build in each field, out would burst a cottontail rabbit from its invisible hiding place, hitting the ground in full stride and bringing Fritz into instant and clamorous pursuit. The scene is indelibly etched in my memory—both Fritz and the rabbit stretched full length in the air and straining every muscle, the rabbit's ears laid back and Fritz's mouth wide open as if ready to gobble up his furry tormentor on the very next stride, even if the rabbit were thirty feet ahead of him.

Then would come a puff of white smoke followed by a satisfying boom, followed sometimes by another— and always bringing that uniquely pungent smell of burning gunpowder. If the rabbit were unhit, Fritz would continue his hot pursuit over the first hill or to the first fence. If the rabbit were hit, Fritz would continue his pursuit

full tilt until scooping up his quarry and crushing its skull. Fritz took no prisoners. Be they slightly crippled, badly crippled, or quadriplegic, Fritz showed no mercy. He had been publicly humiliated too many times by those little cottontailed rodents over the years ever to spare a cripple.

And so it went. One or another of us boys would retrieve each rabbit (Fritz was too proud to fetch and tote), glad to be a productive member of the hunt; and on we would go, through field after field, until Uncle Ott's hunting coat was filled and we each were carrying a satisfying number of our Thanksgiving Day quarry. Every minute had been exciting. Even Daddy was having fun. But it had to end, and by eleven o'clock we were out behind the woodhouse, "cleaning our rabbits." Cottontails are so easy to prepare for the table that it's as if they had built-in zippers. Their skin can be stripped off intact, like a rubber glove, so easily a child can do it; and so we did. As fast as we skinned them, Daddy and Uncle Ott would finish them up, to be washed under the pump and hung on the clothes line to cool and freeze.

Inside the house was every child's dream of Thanksgiving Day. The big dinner was well under way and the kitchen smelled like the pure essence of Thanksgiving. Mother and Aunt Pearlie were bustling around, putting the finishing touches on things, the kitchen windows were steamed up with humidity from the warm, fragrant air, and the air itself was filled with snatches of hunting and cooking conversation, as we washed up at the kitchen stove for dinner.

At last everything was on the dining room table. There were chicken and noodles (the noodles cooked in the creamy chicken broth, along with bits of chicken meat), mashed potatoes, candied sweet potatoes, Aunt Pearlie's famous potato salad, green beans, creamed corn, home-made cottage cheese, stuffed celery, hot biscuits and warm pumpkin pie with our own whipped cream.

But as interesting as the food to us children was the conversation. Uncle Ott was always a convivial guest. He was a natural story-teller with a good voice and infectious laugh. Aunt Pearlie was good at interjecting a word here and there and was generous with her own merry laugh. Our cousin Roger had inherited his father's conversational talents, and our cousin Lois was beautiful and witty; she sometimes chimed in with a laugh like tinkling bells. We children had difficulty in feeling close to Lois because she was older than we and away at school. I remember her mainly as being so well educated and so pretty that I always felt clumsy and tongue-tied in her presence. To my own rather introverted family, isolated as we were on the farm, Thanksgiving dinner was the conversational equivalent of viewing a favorite television program today, but much, much more important because it could happen only once each year rather than daily or weekly.

Uncle Ott, a city mail carrier in the county seat eight miles from our house, was our tour guide to city life. His stories were usually about persons or happenings in town, and it seemed to us that he knew everybody! In fact, over the years of his stories we became so well acquainted with some of his characters that they themselves seemed like old friends. Thanksgiving dinner conversation, in marked contrast to that of our usual meals, would go on for two hours, long after the mashed potatoes were cold and stiff and the gravy covered with wrinkled leather. It could come to an end only when Mother and Aunt Pearlie would insist that they had to get busy at cleaning up the wreckage of the dinner and setting the kitchen in order.

In the remainder of the afternoon Daddy would find some farm chores which needed doing, while we boys would accompany Uncle Ott on another hunt. This time we would look mainly for birds—quail or Hungarian partridge. These hunts were generally not very meat productive, but were more social than in the forenoon. Uncle Ott had a sort of springy, loose-jointed walk which could cover ground at a deceptively high rate. Therefore, we were able to go beyond our own farm and explore some of the neighboring woods and pastures in rambling fashion, unlike in the regimented hunt of the morning. By late afternoon we were back at the house, where we would sit down again for a piece of pumpkin pie and another visit before our relatives would leave for "town."

Before going, Uncle Ott and Roger would bring in from the car armloads of magazines, accumulated since their latest visit. These would include *Colliers, Saturday Evening Post, Liberty, Ladies Home Journal* and *Country Gentleman*. Back in that pre-television era, fiction magazines were favorite home entertainment. Many of the stories were serialized (or at least used the same cast of characters week after week) and we could hardly say good-bye to our relatives before sitting down to read what had been happening to wily old country lawyer Scattergood Baines or equally wily but often inebriate Scottish seafarer Colin Glencannon, in the *Saturday Evening Post*. But say good-bye we would, and as a happy Thanksgiving Day ended, we were already thinking of the next one—assuming with childish immortality that they would go on forever.

CHAPTER XII

THE LITTLE ONE-ROOM SCHOOLHOUSE

All farm children of the twenties probably remember their own little one-room school as being the original, and I am no exception. Green Hill Grade School, Pike Township, Jay County, Indiana truly was the original little red one-room schoolhouse against which all others could be measured; and Green Hill was the perfect name for it.

Framed by farm fields on three sides and a wooded stream bank on the fourth, this sturdy brick structure attracted its grubby little students like a rusty red magnet throughout a radius of two miles. This two-mile limit no doubt was agreed by Township Trustees and the County School Superintendent to be a reasonable walking distance—which it was. I know, because the distance from our house to the school house was exactly two miles, and to this day I am shocked to observe that today's children are reluctant to walk even two blocks to school.

Our schoolhouse, probably thirty feet by forty feet in size, sat at a crossroad in the corner of a tract of land about the size of a football field. Near the south end of the school building was a small coal shed and south of that a small horse stable. Three teeter-totter boards, a slide, a maypole, a water pump and a flagpole completed the improvements except for the two outhouses. These were thoughtfully positioned at opposite corners of the most distant end of the tract.

If I let my memory drift back to the individual or combined smells of cedar oil, chalk dust and unwashed children, the interior of the room comes back in every detail.

Inside the schoolhouse door, on the left was the girls' cloak room and on the right the boys' cloak room. Directly ahead stood a big, pot-bellied iron stove five feet high, with a sheet iron fire screen around all but the front. Rows of desks on wrought iron frames mounted on movable wooden slats filled the room except for the far end. Here was the wall-to-wall blackboard, in front of which was the teacher's chair and desk. Facing the teacher was the "recitation bench," actually a church type of seat. Above one end of the blackboard, on a wall bracket, was a bust of Lincoln; at the other a bust of Washington.

Because one school served all eight grades, and because each grade taught at least "reading, 'riting and 'rithmetic," the recitation bench was the site of continual activity during the school day. The teaching procedure required that each class of each grade be conducted at this bench, which could be literally the hot seat at times, particularly if the seated student were ill prepared. The enrollment of our school varied over the years from a low of sixteen to a high of thirty-five, which, split up over eight grades, made for very small classes per grade. In a two-student class it was difficult for the pupil to escape attention of the teacher, once up there at the bench. It was pretty much a matter of "stand and deliver," or else. Or else was the "hickory stick," in our case a polished hickory pointer, as kept on the teacher's desk or in the teacher's hands and not used exclusively for pointing.

Holding each class at the recitation bench in open forum may seem to readers to have been hopelessly inefficient, but actually had some advantages over the private classroom system. For example, each pupil, if not busy at his or her desk, could hear and observe everything occurring at the front of the room. This would provide a preview of the future for the lower classes and a review of the past for the higher classes. Furthermore, it taught all students to be able to concentrate exclusively on their own lessons if necessary—something important in later life. At the very least, it provided relief from boredom, a common complaint of today's students.

We had a different school teacher for each of my five years at Green Hill in grades one through five. Although this was up to sixty-eight years ago, I remember them well—John McFarland, Gladys McKinley, Roger Haines, Kenneth Schwartz and Bernice Tharp. I have since wondered why none taught consecutive terms at Green Hill. The inference could be that one year of us was enough.

Probably everyone remembers that first day of school, so mine was nothing special. But special enough to me was a new pair of bib overalls with the cuffs turned up about six inches to allow for shrinkage of the denim and for future growth of the wearer. I well remember the impressive rustle those cuffs made as I walked, and the new smell of the fabric. But most of all I remember my first sight of our teacher, John McFarland—tall, thin, Lincolnesque figure in his fifties with a thick moustache and most impressive of all, wearing a wool suit! In a land of bib overalls, the wool-suited man is king. This suit was to be John's uniform throughout the school term, with a brown cardigan sweater added under the jacket in winter. His refined dress, his wire-rimmed spectacles and air of weary confidence somehow were undiminished by the fact that he chewed tobacco at his desk and used a spare coal bucket as a spittoon, or that he drove a horse and buggy each day to and from school. After all, to us snow or mud-bound pedestrians that neat, black buggy and lively bay mare looked like the ultimate in travel luxury.

As can be imagined, John had no trouble in keeping order at Green Hill. He had only to look up from his book or paper, clear his throat and fix his steely glance in space and you could hear a pin drop. Not that any of us would dare to drop one. It was as if he had created education as an extension of himself. School was for schooling, period.

Our other teachers, all newly out of "normal" school, did not have John's iron rule. The women teachers were given by the "big boys" secret disrespectful names, crude and not very imaginative. Gladys McKinley was called of course Gladass, Bernice Tharp, Burnass, and so on. Gladys had a boyfriend named Horace Pratt, who used to stop at the school once in a while to court her. Anybody with a name like "Horace" was already in trouble around school kids of the time, and the most simple and innocent little remarks by Horace were all grist for our crudity mill. But none of this during school hours.

Only once can I remember a real breach of discipline, and this was a major challenge of power by an eighth grade boy, big for his age and old for his grade. His name I don't recall, but I think he refused to clean erasers for our teacher, Roger Haines. Things quickly went from vocal threats to physical threats, and soon he and Roger were locked in a test of physical strength in the open space at one end of the recitation bench and teacher's desk. Their grunting and straining quickly drew an appreciative but silent ringside attendance, although I remember being embarrassed by this naked challenge of establishment regulations. It was my first exposure to anarchy.

Roger Haines had one lame hand as a result of infantile paralysis, and for this reason his adult strength was offset to the point that it was an even match. The struggle lasted several minutes, on and off the floor, knocking over the recitation bench, the waste paper basket and skewing the teacher's desk and nearby rows of seats. At last, apparently by tacit agreement, hostilities ceased, with much brushing of clothes, tucking of shirt tails and general huffings and puffings. I do not remember any apologies from either party, nor do I remember any evidence of continued resentment, although there must have been some.

This is the only hostile act I can remember in student-teacher relationship, and in fact, fights even between students were not common. We did, however, have a very active outdoor recreation program. Program is not really the word. In fact, our games were about as unprogrammed as games can get, the big three being black man, stink base and fox and geese.

Fox and geese is the only one of these games (or at least the only one of the names) which I have ever heard mentioned outside of Green Hill. The way we played it was to trample a wagon wheel pattern into the snow, then station the fox at the hub, while the gaggle of geese occupied the rim. The fox was at liberty to attempt to capture geese at will, as long as he followed the trampled paths. Likewise the geese could flee, but only by following the trampled rim or spokes. A goose, if captured, then became the fox, which practice does not have much in common with real life.

Stink base, intriguing though the name sounds, was a sort of dry land substitute for fox and geese, with two main bases serving to control the traffic. It had the added feature that it was a contest between two sides, and those captured were placed in isolation on the stink base, the object being to deplete the enemy forces. The name surely must be local, as I have never heard it used in other parts of the world.

Black man (this was before political correctness) was our favorite, as it provided almost unrestricted liberty for open field running. Essentially there were only two bases, each about a hundred feet long, with about a hundred feet between them. The black man had his own small base in the middle and had to stay on it until one or more of those on line would attempt to change sides. Then he was free to run and grab any quarry he could catch. A simple tag did not count. He had to catch and hold the runner. This made it a contact sport and created opportunity for interplay between boys and girls. An even more interesting version of the game permitted the appointment of an assistant, a sort of deputy who could throw and hold a runner until officially tagged by the black man. At the time the name of the game seemed unquestionable to me, but at the present writing it makes no sense at all.

In addition to playing these games, we did a lot of fishing, particularly in the springtime. We were fortunate to have the Little Salamonia River flowing through the Kaderly place, immediately below the west end of the school grounds. So at noon we would take our dinner buckets with us, hurry down to the "crick," get a favorite willow pole out of hiding and eat our sandwiches while waiting for a cork to bob. We caught sunfish, catfish, suckers, red horse, and shiners, though what we did with them I can't remember. I do remember, however, that even after the school bell had brought us back to our lessons, I could still hear the murmur of the water, the throbbing song of robins and smell the rich earthy odors of springtime along the crick—and the fishy odor on my hands.

Green Hill was not big on organized sports, and in fact, until Kenneth Woods joined our student body we ignored such activities. A year or two before our last year at Green Hill, however, the Woods family moved into the house at the end of our lane, and Kenneth became a pupil at our school. Kenneth was not a farm kid. He was from Petoskey, Michigan, and brought with him what we regarded as city ways. Instead of wearing overalls, he wore pants and sweaters. He even wore woolen scarfs around his neck. Instead of a Karo bucket, he had a full-size, regulation black lunch box with a Thermos bottle section. Instead of walking with us to school, he rode a fine bicycle in warm weather and skied to school in winter. He had a basketball, a football and of course a baseball, and so became the pitcher of our quickly organized baseball team. My own service on the team lasted only about three innings, all on second base, where I spent my time hoping nobody would hit a fly in my direction. About the third inning Kenneth hurled a fast one at me from the pitcher's box as a kind of routine morale builder as in big league warm-ups. But I was thinking of other things and the baseball hit me squarely in one eye, putting me out of the game and to my relief, off the team.

At the opposite end of the student body spectrum, farthest removed from Kenneth Woods, was Billy Kemp. I remember the day Billy first showed up to enter the second or third grade. Billy was a short, chunky kid, with a flat happy face, round eyes and a permanent cowlick all around his forehead, which gave him a curiously startled expression. He was from what today's sociologists would call an underprivileged family, but Billy never knew it. Billy never knew much about hygiene or handkerchiefs either and wiped his nose, always running, on his sweater sleeves. As a result, from wrist to shoulder his sweater sleeves always glistened, like the pathway of garden slugs.

Because Billy was literally the new kid on the block and had no siblings in school to defend him, he was the uncomplaining butt of every low trick the big boys could dream up. Snipe-hunting would have been made to order for Billy, but too elaborate for the occasion. Instead, he was handed such jobs as putting the odd toad down a girl's neck, or delivering a paper bag of horse apples to the teacher. The one which sets some kind of record is the time Ora Kaderly, from inside the coal house, conned Billy, on the outside, into putting his pecker through a knothole, whereon Ora stretched it and hooked it behind a bent nail on the inside. So there was poor Billy, flattened up against the coal house, unable to move much except his face, which was contorted into all sorts of piteous pleadings; and there was Ora, like a sideshow barker, exhorting passersby to come see the show, girls and all. Shortly after I came on this scene, a motherly eighth grade girl unhooked little Billy from his unique tether, and I remember him ruefully but gratefully inspecting himself for damage, then going on about school-yard activities with no particular complaints. Billy was a rock. I wonder where he is today and if he has a handkerchief.

Formal sex education, of course, did not exist in our school, but we did our best to improvise—at least we boys did. Every scrap of such information, no matter how wildly erroneous, was cycled and recycled endlessly. For example, it was from the "big boys" at Green Hill that I first learned that oriental girls are anatomically different from white girls. "Aw, come on! How do you know?" "Everybody knows; and besides, didn't you ever notice their eyes?" And so another piece of that mysterious jigsaw puzzle of the opposite sex was discovered and fitted into place—albeit "crossways."

An aid in field observation was the fact the out-houses were located at the brink of the wooded hill at the remote end of the school yard. We boys found we could hide there in the bushes behind the girls' outhouse and listen to what the girls had to say; it wasn't long before we found that one of the boards at the back could be pried off and thus provide visual access. However, this situation was too good to last. One of the smallest boys, not fully appreciative of what we had going for us there, could not resist jabbing a stick up through our peep hole, thus blowing our cover forever. From then on the girls would post a guard on the outside.

Although we boys at age nine or ten were not above using a more direct, hands-on approach in our field study, this was not very successful either. For one thing it was rarely that we had the opportunity to ambush a girl out of earshot of a call for help. Another problem was that they all wore long underwear, opening only in a drop seat at the back, and everything seemed to be pinned to something else with safety pins. Do-it-yourself sex education had its limitations at Green Hill.

So what did we learn inside the schoolhouse? We learned many things. We had a rather full curriculum, actually. We studied grammar, literature, history, geography, arithmetic, physiology, writing—all kinds of things. Knowing that there were going to be only two or three of us up there at the recitation bench at a time was a real inducement to study. We had very frequent spelling bees and "ciphering" contests and much memorizing of classical poetry. From a practical standpoint our curriculum and the results obtained no doubt were superior to those of the average grade school today.

Probably the best day of school was Christmas program day. In fact, for an entire week or two after the Christmas decorations had been put up, school was the place to be. I was surprised and amazed each year by the transformation which could be created by draping green and red ribbons of crepe paper from all sides of the room to a central focal point, culminating in the big red folding bell! We always had a decorated Christmas tree and spent weeks working on a Christmas program to be given on the last evening before closing for Christmas vacation. This was a chance to show off in front of our parents (and that secret special person in the student body).

On entering the building on the big night, we knew our dreams were realized. Could this lamp-lighted palace of glittering tinsel and bells actually be our dumb old schoolroom? Everywhere at our own desks were chattering parents and pre-schoolers, all dressed up and eagerly awaiting the big Christmas program which we had been rehearsing for weeks. But despite repeated rehearsal, no program was without its casualties. Notable among these was the time Velda May hit a complete blackout. I can see him yet looking down at the floor, then up to the ceiling, scratching his head, then blurting out "So this is Christmas Eve—er—so this is Christmas Eve—er," then wheeling and disappearing behind the curtain, never to return. The strange thing about it is that the line he stammered out was not even in his part.

At the end of the show the Christmas "treats" were passed out, one to each student. These were identical from year to year, as if specified by the county school superintendent. This long-dreamed-of treat was a small paper poke containing one orange, a peppermint cane, some "chocolate drops" and some gum drops. It was wonderful!

The program over, and treats in hand, we trooped to our 1919 Ford and headed for home, still made starry-eyed by the stage door glamour and excitement of the evening. That night in bed, before going to sleep, we thought of nothing but Christmas vacation ahead, with its own Sunday School treat, and of Christmas morning presents and Christmas dinner, long days of sledding on the hill and skating on the creek. Life was perfect then and would never change.

Following Christmas vacation, life at school settled down to the long haul through the tunnel of winter; but always with us was the knowledge that at the end of this tunnel was the light of summer vacation.

Actually school at Green Hill was not unpleasant. It is true that walking through deep snow was sometimes a struggle, but it was also kind of romantic, bringing daydreams right out of James Oliver Curwood's books of the Far North. The snow also brought in "fox and geese" on the playground and sledding on the hill leading down to the creek. It also brought skating on the creek, which was one of our favorites. One reason we liked it was because of the peril involved. There were always open water holes at the riffles and sagging and creaking thin ice in places, depending on the weather. But if the "ice was on," the noon dinner hour would always find us on the creek.

I remember one time along toward spring when our favorite skating place was covered by about an inch of melt water, and when Dewey Smith, quick to assess the potential of the situation, methodically chopped a sharp slot across the skating route. Then along came Dorothy Kaderly in a ratty brown fur coat, skimming along with her hands clasped behind her, completely unaware of Dewey's nefarious trap. When she hit the notch, she did a belly smacker on the flooded ice and continued to shoot forward pushing a bow wave ahead of her chin, looking for all the world like a swimming muskrat, in her brown fur coat.

As winter drew to a close, our walk to school was not

immediately made easier because when the frost went out of the ground we fought mud and ruts instead of snow. But soon the warm winds of spring were to come and with them the road grader, magically transforming deep ruts into a broad ribbon of brown clay and gravel and bringing smooth and easy walking. Along with the road grader came the birds—robins, bluebirds, meadowlarks, orioles and bob-o-links. That wonderful day, "last day of school" was at hand.

The annual last day of school rivals Christmas in memory, probably because it presaged even better things to come. It was the fulfillment of countless deskbound hours of daydreaming while staring through the schoolhouse windows to the beckoning fields and woods outside. It was the open door to that wondrous world of summer vacation. The day itself was notable more for what it meant was coming, rather than for what it was, being an abbreviated school day, with review of test papers and handing out of grades. Not much work was done.

Because the last day came in early April, it traditionally opened the barefoot season, and therefore on leaving the schoolhouse door we would sit down near the tee-ter-totters and remove our shoes and stockings. We would then stuff the stockings into the shoes, tie the laces together and with the shoes slung around our necks and our books swinging from book straps, head for home. Little did we know that absolutely never in later life would we be able to experience the feeling of utter bliss and contentment that was ours as we four siblings made our barefooted way home from Green Hill on that ultimate last day of school back in April, 1927. We were never again to attend our one-room Green Hill School. The next year, as a first step toward growing up, we would be transferred to the much larger Madison Township Consolidated School on our way out into the world.

CHAPTER XIII

MOTHER AND DADDY

Daddy shaved once a week—on Sunday morning before dressing for church. I can see him as if it were yesterday, with his shirt off and only one suspender of his bib overalls buckled, stropping his bone-handled razor on the razor strop, which was suspended from the first clothes hook of the row of hooks behind the kitchen door. On a kitchen chair beside him would be spread one page of the newspaper, and on the newspaper a steaming washpan of water from the reservoir of the kitchen range. Beside the washpan was his shaving mug, containing a badger-bristled shaving brush and a piece of soap. All this was arranged in front of a cheap, oak-framed mirror, suspended from a nail on the kitchen wall. This was the only mirror we ever used—the "dressing mirror" for the entire family.

After stropping his razor, first on the rough strop, then on the smooth strop, he would wash his face and neck with the "washrag," then work up a foamy lather in the mug and brush it thickly on his face; and here the really interesting part (for us children) would begin. With each stroke a swath of heavy, brown stubble would disappear, leaving smooth, pink skin.

Daddy was only five-feet, six-inches tall, but he had broad shoulders and giant biceps, and it was as he posed there in front of that eighteen by twenty-four inch mirror hanging from the kitchen wall that he seemed his most impressive. With his feet in heavy work shoes firmly planted on the floor, his left fist planted on his hip for stability, and

his right arm raised and angled to bring the razor to his face, he reminded me of a heroic statue—or at least the Arm and Hammer Baking Soda trademark.

At the end of each two or three audible strokes, he would carefully wipe the razor on the edge of the newspaper, leaving a blob of white lather mixed with brown whiskers. And at the end of the shave, these blobs would remain in a neat row, and Daddy's face would emerge clean and pink and ten years younger. Shaving seemed to rejuvenate not only his appearance, but also his spirits, and while preparing for the operation he usually would be humming snatches of the "Old Rugged Cross" or "Bringing in the Sheaves," no doubt thinking of church service to come. When finished shaving, Daddy would squeeze out the washrag, hang it on the binder twine line above the stove, empty the washpan in the sink on the back porch, put his razor back in its case and up on the top of the cabinet, then carefully fold up the newspaper with its week's crop of whiskers and stuff it into the kitchen range. This was a ritual he followed meticulously, never leaving any clean-up work for Mother or anyone else to do. Whether it be shaving or any other chore around the farm, he always finished every job and put every tool back in place.

Daddy lived a truly Christian life. He did not try to press his beliefs on others but was a devoted Christian himself. He believed the Bible literally and lived by the Ten Commandments, although he did it so quietly and privately that it simply seemed like the right thing to do— and odd that not everybody did likewise. It was not until we children were long away from home that we realized what remarkable strength of character he possessed and how fortunate we were to have been exposed to his example.

But Daddy was human, and although he was tolerant of the shortcomings of people, he expected perhaps too much of his other friends the farm animals. Or maybe he took too literally the "man shall have dominion" passage in the Bible. At any rate, after training a horse or a cow to do something right, he expected this lesson to be remembered for life; if it were not, he could be rather vigorous in administering a refresher course. During these retraining sessions, we children learned to give him lots of space.

One of these sessions I can remember is the time when our oldest brother Charles was only eight or nine and was put up on one of our horses, Maud, to guide her between the rows of the "truck patch," while Daddy would operate the "one horse" cultivator drawn behind her. Maud, used to working in tandem with her more intelligent team mate, Molly, made the mistake of shying at something, causing Daddy to plow out a row of potatoes, and worse yet almost throwing Charles under her feet.

Without giving her a second chance to do the right thing, Daddy lifted Charles off the poor horse, unhooked the traces and led Maud behind him while he looked for something with which to enforce his commands. Seeing our abandoned baseball bat nearby, he picked it up and climbing on poor old Maud's back, said to her "Now let's go walk that row again." He then took her down the same row from which she had bolted, whacking her first on one side of the head, then the other with our baseball bat until it broke in two. Reversing the splintered bat handle, he continued his lesson, using the handle on her ears, until both he and Maud were pretty well settled down. Then he put Charles back on, this time himself leading Maud around for a while before hitching up the plow. And the lesson worked. Maud, although afraid to step out more than six inches at a time, managed to finish the cultivating without further incident.

These flights of temper were rare, and I relate this one mainly as the exception to the rule. But now the thought of one other comes to mind. This one, which my brother Robbie and I have often laughed about, happened in the cow stable while we were milking our Jersey cows. In those days there were no milking machines and milking twice daily could be a time-consuming chore, particularly if several milk cows were involved. At the time of this incident we were milking twelve to fifteen cows, each one of which had her own personality and her own ideas about this invasion of privacy. And so it became necessary to train each cow to try to be cooperative and considerate about the process in order to get the job done in timely and sanitary fashion.

Some cows seemed to be instinctively thoughtful and understanding, while others seemed to be instinctively resentful and distrusting. In order to safely milk the latter type it was necessary to use kicking chains, designed something like manacles, fitting over the achilles tendons of the cow's hind legs, and locking their legs together. This is all well and good except that sometimes a particularly ornery cow could get off one good shot at the milker as he was crouched down alongside her heels preparing to put the cuffs in place. And this is what happened to Daddy.

Robbie and I heard this explosion at the far end of the stable and could not resist standing up far enough to peer down the row of cows to watch. Daddy never, never used any profanity at all, but always kept up a running monologue of threats and admonitions, as he reasoned with, in this case, the bovine offender. After giving her a couple rights to the abdomen with his fist, he then resorted to using his feet (we learned later that he had broken a bone in his fist), kicking her audibly in the stomach. In self- defense of her stomach, the poor cow quickly lay down on the stable floor, whereupon Daddy immediately climbed on top of her and commenced jumping up and down on her recumbent body. He always wore Sears and Roebuck's super- grade, triple-soled, cordovan horsehide work shoes, that with repeated wetting and drying had turned up at the toes, giving them a kind of elfin look. The memory of this grown man grimly and energetically jumping up and down on a cow is a cartoon-like picture I will never forget. Eventually Daddy ran out of breath and resentment and had to make his way through the stanchions and up in front of the cow to talk her to her feet, whereupon he resumed milking. She didn't kick him again for a long time. Not a word ever was said about this incident at the time, nor later, although it must have been difficult for Daddy to finish his share of the milking with a broken metacarpal bone in his right hand.

I feel disloyal about having written the above, because Daddy really was a kind and gentle person, as one must be to care for all the horses, cows, sheep, pigs and chickens which we had around the farm back in those days. This burden of intensive and diversified livestock and grain farming was not made any easier by the fact that the farm, during the entire twenty-three-year span from World War I to World War II, carried a heavy mortgage. This mortgage was a continual worry to Daddy. And then, of course, the Great Depression of the thirties didn't help matters.

Daddy was pretty inventive about devising ways to

try to augment our cash income. Around 1924, when we four children would have been seven, eight, nine and ten years old, respectively, he conceived the notion of putting in a commercial strawberry patch. This sounded great to us kids until that first shipment of strawberry plants arrived by freight from Michigan, and we had to start planting them in rows so long they seemed to disappear on the horizon. Although these rows reached our childhood horizon, they were actually only 660 feet long. I suppose there were about a dozen rows, which would be at least an acre of strawberries. This acre we kids planted as an introduction to intensive, cash-crop farming. And little did we know that planting was actually the fun part.

Hoeing strawberries to a kid must rank right up there with what rowing a ship was to a galley slave. There was no end to it. By the time we finished one hoeing, along would come a thunderstorm, soaking the ground, and as soon as it had dried out for a day, it needed hoeing again. When the runners spread out to cover the ground, the hoeing operation was replaced by hand weeding. But the following year the worst was yet to come, when we would be hoeing the new patch while picking the old patch.

To his credit, Daddy would pitch in and help us whenever he possibly could, and he could literally make the dirt fly with a hoe, causing us to lean on our own hoes to watch him in astonishment. He was equally good at picking and seemed to make the berries almost jump into the baskets, as he shuffled his strong stubby fingers through the thick foliage of the berry row. As an incentive to picking, we kids were given one cent per quart. Considering that the berries sold at only ten cents per quart, this was a ten percent commission, and we were quite pleased by the arrangement. No doubt today's sociologists, politicians and TV anchor persons would look on the strawberry venture as being a particularly vile example of child exploitation, if not downright child abuse. However, we did not resent it one bit and it certainly was good for us, in preparation for life in general. The strawberry business lasted only three years, by which time we were old enough to be useful in more important aspects of farm life and labor.

For every ounce of effort Daddy asked of us kids, he gave a pound of his own. Winter or summer he was out of bed by 4:00 a.m., building a fire in the kitchen range so it would be ready to cook breakfast. Then, if field work were in season, he would go to the pasture and bring up the horses, feed them, and feed the cows and hogs. Only then, after having done two hours work would he return to the house, make coffee, and begin to awaken the rest of the family.

In winter he would go through the same routine, up at 4:00, build the fire, feed horses, cows, sheep and hogs, everything except the chickens; and until the time that we children were old enough to help, he would even do the milking before awakening the family. During lambing time he would be bringing up baby lambs to the house at this early morning hour, so that by the time the family was up there would be lambs all over the kitchen. Some would be in the woodbox, or even half in and half out of the oven on a bed of burlap bags, and with milk heating in a nippled bottle standing in a pan of water on the stove. In order to keep up this pace, he used to go to bed at 8:00 or 9:00 p.m. and have a thirty-minute nap at noon. Daddy's inflexible 4:00 a.m. arising schedule became so ingrained in my memory of him that once when he was in his seventies and

I learned that he was then "sleeping in" until 7:30, I felt somehow let down, as if a part of my childhood trust had been betrayed.

About the same time Daddy put us to work in the strawberry patch, he also conceived of the idea of running a custom hatchery for baby chicks. For this he ordered an incubator, which although set up in the garage was our most impressive piece of furniture. Why it was done in highly polished, chinese lacquer style I do not know, but there it stood, about the size of two grand pianos and to us just as beautiful. It was seven trays deep, and the top trays were filled with eggs first. Then after three days these trays were moved down to second position, and a new batch of eggs was put in the top position, and so on. At the end of twenty-one days the chicks from the first trays would hatch out at the bottom position, with a new hatch coming off every three days from then on. In addition to his farm work, Daddy used to run this incubator entirely himself, and although I think it was modestly successful, it did not lift the mortgage. But it did assure that we would have a continually renewed supply of hundreds of cute, fluffy little baby chicks cheeping away all spring long in big, flat, perforated boxes marked "LIVE BABY CHICKS." It assured also that we would raise a thousand young White Leghorns every summer for our eating and selling flock and keep three-hundred laying hens almost year around for egg money.

But the main business of our farm was corn and hog growing, with wheat, oats, soybeans and sometimes barley as other grains. During the period when we children were old enough to work in the fields yet were still at home, say from age ten to twenty, Daddy rented additional land

and expanded the herds. During this period we were farming around two-hundred acres and milking fifteen Jersey cows, lambing and shearing over one-hundred breeding ewes, keeping seven or eight brood sows yielding fifty or more feeder pigs, and of course putting up all our own hay and corn fodder, and all this with five horses and no tractor or electrical power. Daddy managed all this with no family friction or argument whatsoever. This speaks volumes about him, it seems to me now, although we children did not really appreciate how remarkable he was.

Unlike Daddy, Mother was not a mover and shaker but she was every child's idea of what a mother should be—a dispenser of sympathy and kindness and a provider of an endless supply of great things to eat. In the latter category, Mother was without peer.

I can still see her baking an angel food cake, one of her specialities. I can see her sifting Swan's Down cake flour five times onto newspaper spread on the tattered oilcloth of the kitchen table, and remember wondering where the lumps were that she seemed to be trying to sift out. She was so expert at separating the whites from the yokes of thirteen eggs that it was fascinating to watch. Never did she break a yolk, passing them back and forth between the shell halves. Cream-of-tartar never looked like cream to me, and to this day I don't know what tartar is. But it worked, and the egg whites, under Mother's gentle hands, supported the flour and sugar in a light feathery batter which always turned out of that three-legged pan true to its name—angel food, although I do not remember any angels around our house to eat it—except maybe Mother.

She was equally adept at making devil's food cake,

sponge cake, and what she called "just white cake" and "just yellow cake." In fact, it is difficult to picture her other than in an apron, and either peering into the oven or using the tail of her apron for a pot holder to slide a cake pan or cookie sheet in or out of the open over door—sugar cookies, gingerbread cookies, peanut butter cookies and most often of all, molasses cookies—probably because we had so much home-grown sorghum molasses around. Memory tells me that when I had first learned to read well enough to appreciate books, my happiest hours centered around the big chair near the "base burner" in the winter time with a new book and with a three-inch stack of molasses cookies on the arm of the chair. Under those circumstances, the most bland adventures of even the Bobbsey Twins were exciting.

Mother was a genius at converting fresh fruit into pies. She had only to say, "If you will go pick some transparent apples, I will bake some open apples pies," to get instant action; or strawberries, raspberries, blackberries, cherries—anything ending in "ies," would send us kids out to the patch or orchard. Blackberry pie was my own personal favorite, and much as I feared and detested those huge black-and-yellow-striped spiders which hung out in the blackberry bushes, I would willingly pick blackberries for Mother's pies. She always made them just perfect—not too runny and not too stiff—just oozy enough to cover your tongue with that delectable creamy mixture of blackberry essence and rich flaky crust for which there is no counterpart in today's plastic world.

But Mother was much, much more than the perfect cook, she was that cheerful, helpful, understanding and forgiving person who was always available around the house to cheer, help, understand and forgive those who needed her. She had a good voice (the only one in the family) and often sang little bits of songs while working. She also played the piano, which made her especially popular in our music-starved environs. I can still hear her playing and singing from sheet music such nice old things as "Alice Blue Gown," "They'll Never Believe Me," "Jeanie With the Light Brown Hair," "When You and I Were Young," and my favorite which I can only name "Ben Bolt," which said "Don't you remember sweet Alice, Ben Bolt? Sweet Alice whose hair was so brown. Who wept with delight when you gave her a smile and trembled in tears at your frown." Over and over again I heard Mother play and sing that song, and I always tried to picture a person who could be so mean to sweet Alice as that awful Ben Bolt. And to this day, it bothers me that he could get away with it, if in fact he did.

Mother's sphere of activity was confined mainly to the house, although between herself and us children, Daddy was relieved of most of the chicken-related chores. She also liked to garden, but was not really strong enough to make it work. Every spring Daddy would plow and harrow the vegetable garden for her, and she would seed radishes, lettuce, peas, beets, green beans etc. but as soon as hot weather caught up to her, the weeds caught up to her plantings. It was the same with flowers. Mother loved flowers, but we did not have many flower beds around, because she was not really able to take care of them.

One of Mother's strong points was her feeling for sewing and needlework. Her foot-treadle Singer sewing machine was permanently set up in the dining room, and there she could be found most of the time when not in the kitchen. She could make her way easily through the mystery of "patterns," and I can even now hear the companionable "crump, crump . . ." of her scissors as they resonated on the table boards when she cut cloth pinned on patterns and spread on the dining room table; and I can hear her speaking to us through pins in her mouth, or while biting the thread off a spool. She enjoyed the companionable work of quilting and comfort-making with neighbors and relatives and was good at it. She sometimes selected newly-shorn wool fleeces from our flock at shearing time, to be used later in making comforts for our beds.

Mother was "nice looking," but we children never thought much about whether she would be considered pretty. I do remember that on my first day of entry into the sixth grade of our new school, after leaving our one-room Green Hill, there was a teacher who apparently had known Mother as a girl. When he was reading the roster and came to my name, he gave me a peculiar look and asked if my mother's name was Ethel. When I said it was, he gazed pensively out the window for a moment before going back to the roster. So at home that evening I told Mother I had met her old "beau" Clarence McLaughlin. She kind of blushed and looked at Daddy, then said only that she "used to know him."

Because Mother was always so cheerful and busy inside the house, it never occurred to us children to wonder why she did not run or play outside with us. I remember one time when I started to chase her for something out on the lawn and she playfully started to run, then after only a few steps suddenly sobered, and went abruptly inside. Forty years too soon came the time when we all were sick with scarlet fever except Daddy, and during the night we heard the voice of Dr. Kidder downstairs. Early the next morning, Daddy came up to tell us that Mother was no longer with us. She was only thirty-seven years old, and I had just turned fourteen. Only years later did we piece together that she must have suffered heart damage from a condition which in those days was called "uremic poisoning," which was associated with the birth of our sister Jean, last of Mother's brood. It probably did not help that we all four were born within a space of four and one-half years.

In writing this it occurs to me that I never heard Mother and Daddy exchange a single cross or unkind word with each other. Not one.

EPILOGUE

TIME: 65 Years Later
PLACE: Portland, Indiana COMMERCIAL REVIEW
          News Article, November 8, 1989
          Jack Ronald, Editor

RURAL LAND BECOMING MAN'S DREAM FOREST

Louis Bibler is a patient man.

He knows his dream won't come true for hundreds of years, but he's fulfilled knowing that the seed has been planted.

Or, more accurately, the seeds have been planted. Hundreds of thousands of them. Seeds by the pound. Seeds for "every tree I've ever heard of growing in Indiana," said Bibler.

Bibler, now a resident of Kalispell, Montana, seeded, with the help of his brother Paul, about half of a 55-acre parcel of ground in Pike Township with at least 30 different varieties of hardwood trees and shrubs Saturday. The other half is already new growth of trees and shrubs.

Left alone, the acreage will slowly grow into woodland, and will culminate in the climax forest of Louis Bibler's dreams.

And leaving it alone is precisely what Bibler plans to do. The land, which Bibler and his brother Paul purchased from Jay County farmer Don Coy, will be donated in its entirety to an Indiana tax-exempt, non-profit corporation known as Acres Inc.

Acres, similar in many ways to the nationally-known

Nature Conservancy, was organized in 1960 and focuses its wildlife preservation efforts in northeastern Indiana. It now oversees 17 nature preserves in the northeast corner of the state.

So why does a man from Montana purchase land in Jay County, seed it in trees, and give it away?

Because it used to be home.

"The tract which we purchased this spring includes the creek, woods, and pasture portion of the C. E. Bibler family farm where my two older brothers Charles and Paul, younger sister Jean, and I were born and raised to adulthood," Bibler said. "Our happiest days of childhood were spent along the (Little Salmonie) creek or roaming the woods and pasture of this farm, when all our world was young and new."

For Bibler, last weekend's planting trip was a remarkable homecoming. A 1933 graduate of Madison High School, he'd joined the army in 1941. After the service, he went to college in Seattle, Wash., and embarked upon a career as a geologist, working in the oil fields of the American West and Canada.

He hadn't been home to Jay County for 46 years.

"I had a continual lump in my throat for two days," he said. "Every little detail came back."

Bibler had been planning the project for about 10 years, looking for a way to preserve the natural beauty of his boyhood home. Acres, which limits use of its preserves to hikers and photographers, provided the perfect vehicle. No picnicking, camping, hunting, motorized vehicles or fires are permitted on Acres preserves. There are trails, and visitors are welcome. But the rule "take only pictures and memories, leave only footprints" applies.

Ted Heemstra of Acres was on hand for Saturday's planting, as was Bibler's brother Paul, now a resident of Hood River, Oregon. Charles Bibler, who has been ill, also resides in Montana. Bibler's sister Jean now lives in Urbana, Ill.

"Don Coy kindly agreed to disc (the seeds) in for us," Bibler said. "Everything went according to plan. We got it all done in one day."

Now all his dream needs is time.